Discovering the Richest of Life's Lessons . . .

"Mortality should make us think. Some serious, clarifying questions arise: Against the reality of life's limits, and in view of its preciousness, just how much is enough money? Am I as satisfied, truly satisfied, as I am prosperous? How consequential to me is acclaim or power? Am I gaining as much wisdom as stress from my job? Would disloyalty to my life's partner really accomplish something worthwhile for me? Is my ego serving me well, or am I serving it in blasts of vanity or self-importance? Do I share as many values with my family as I do valuables? Am I developing a meaningful legacy for people who will one day remember me? In short, mortality asks: What is important?"

In *The Path of the Soul*, Rabbi Ben Kamin shows us how we can put life and death into perspective by choosing, creating, and clarifying the basic values that help us live more complete and enriching lives. By embracing mortality, we gain humility, tolerance, harmony, and peace—and the power to transform our lives.

RABBI BEN KAMIN is senior rabbi at the Temple-Tifereth Israel, a 150-year-old Reform congregation in Cleveland, Ohio. He is the author of *Raising a Thoughtful Teenager*, which is also available in a Plume edition, and *Thinking Passover*, available from Dutton. Rabbi Kamin is a regular contributor to the *Cleveland Plain Dealer*.

ALSO BY RABBI BEN KAMIN

Stones in the Soul:
One Day in the Life of an American Rabbi

Raising a Thoughtful Teenager:
A Book of Answers and Values for Parents

Thinking Passover:
A Rabbi's Book of Holiday Values

The Path of the Soul

—∞∞—

Making Peace with Mortality

Rabbi Ben Kamin

A PLUME BOOK

PLUME
Published by the Penguin Group
Penguin Putnam Inc., 375 Hudson Street, New York, New York 10014, U.S.A.
Penguin Books Ltd, 27 Wrights Lane, London W8 5TZ, England
Penguin Books Australia Ltd, Ringwood, Victoria, Australia
Penguin Books Canada Ltd, 10 Alcorn Avenue, Toronto, Ontario, Canada M4V 3B2
Penguin Books (N.Z.) Ltd, 182–190 Wairau Road, Auckland 10, New Zealand

Penguin Books Ltd, Registered Offices: Harmondsworth, Middlesex, England

First published by Plume, a member of Penguin Putnam Inc.

First Printing, August, 1999
10 9 8 7 6 5 4 3 2

Excerpt from "Kisses, Can You Come Back Like Ghosts?" in *Honey and Salt*,
copyright © 1963 by Carl Sandburg and renewed 1991 by Margaret
Sandburg, Helga Sandburg Crile and Janet Sandburg. Reprinted by
permission of Harcourt Brace & Company.

 REGISTERED TRADEMARK—MARCA REGISTRADA

LIBRARY OF CONGRESS CATALOGING-IN-PUBLICATION DATA:
Kamin, Ben.
    The path of the soul : making peace with mortality / Ben Kamin.
    p.   cm.
    ISBN 0-452-28093-1
    1. Death—Religious aspects—Judaism.   2. Death—Psychological aspects.
3. Spiritual life—Judaism.   I. Title.
BM635.4.K36   1999
296.3'3—dc21   98-49652
                                                                        CIP

Printed in the United States of America
Set in Weiss
Designed by Julian Hamer

BOOKS ARE AVAILABLE AT QUANTITY DISCOUNTS WHEN USED TO PROMOTE PRODUCTS
OR SERVICES. FOR INFORMATION PLEASE WRITE TO PREMIUM MARKETING DIVISION,
PENGUIN PUTNAM INC., 375 HUDSON STREET, NEW YORK, NEW YORK 10014.

To the Memory of Martin J. Rosen
"Come on in, Benjel. Tell me what's happening."

CONTENTS

ACKNOWLEDGMENTS

I am grateful for the work that I do, in which the lives and prayers of congregants are so often revealed to me. This is a great responsibility, and I acknowledge that in this book, such lives are occasionally revealed. In some cases, I have used fictitious names in order to maintain privacy.

The character named Emma Bennett, who appears throughout this book, is based upon the real life of M. R. Berger. I am indebted to M. R.'s husband, Jerry, as well as other members of her family, for sharing her story with me. May her memory always be for blessing.

I wish to thank a number of people who have been generous with their time and helpful with their suggestions, reading and reviewing the manuscript, enlightening me with their insights. These include Susan Belman, Crickett Karson, Dr. Howard Ross, Dr. Brian Berman, and Professor Michael Cook. Sharon Beckett has been invaluable with investigation, evaluation, and considered suggestions. Debra Kamin has assisted me with information and research—especially regarding the Mexican custom of The Day of the Dead.

I am thankful for a long and wonderful partnership with Deb Brody, my editor and teacher. We have produced books and a splendid friendship. Meanwhile, I remain thankful and joyous that Faith Hamlin, my literary agent, continues to believe in me and to share her good spirits with my family and me.

I thank goodness that Cathy is my wife and that Sari and Debra are my daughters. They are the coordinates of my life on this earth.

—⊰ෙ৩ঌ৩ঌ৩ঌ৩ঌঌঌ——

A Time to Live, a Time to Die

It was one night many years ago when I saw the effect of mortality for the first time, during an otherwise celebratory occasion—a wedding banquet for the children of good friends of my parents. Many of the members of the small congregation to which my family belonged were present at this emotional gathering of hard-working people who had shared much together over the years.

Midway through the evening, a hush began to spread through the room. The rabbi of the congregation was coming to pay a visit, and he was bringing his wife along. She had not been seen much around the community because she was ill with cancer. The arrival of Rabbi Mond and his wife was of particular interest to us youngsters who had otherwise been preoccupied with loud music, pizza appetizers, and the opposite sex.

As it turned out, the adults in the room knew that Rabbi and Mrs. Mond were coming to say good-bye. The Monds had been with us for just four years and were well liked. Sally Mond, however, wanted to return to her native Australia in order to die there. Many people at that wedding party, including the gracious parents of the bride, knew this. The parents had invited the rabbi and his wife for the whole evening, but the Monds wanted to just stop by and not intrude upon a happy occasion with their anguish.

Rabbi Mond, who had already accepted a teaching position in Australia, suddenly appeared on the podium where the band now stopped playing. I saw that his blue eyes glistened. A big, strapping man in his late forties, he nervously stroked his prematurely graying beard. He was saying something about affection and bonds and milestones that he would now miss, when a ghost appeared from behind him.

Sally Mond was creamy white and drawn. Her smile at first frightened us; there seemed to be no breath moving through her mouth, and her teeth barely clung to her gums. Someone behind me whispered that she had always been such a pleasant-looking woman. The large rabbi held her hand but it looked as though he could have lifted his wife in one palm. Mrs. Mond wore a wig that was already tipped in the direction of eternity. Some people sobbed in the room but most were spellbound. During what had been a celebration of life, we were all confronted with the reality of mortality.

Sally Mond floated toward the microphone. Her husband hovered behind her, immense, yet tender. She stood erect, however, and we realized that her eyes still shone with life. Her sad smile came through and she spoke one sentence: "I am grateful for what I have had, and accept what will be." She then bowed her head slightly in the direction of the mesmerized bride and groom and disappeared behind her husband. The space that the two visitors occupied was quickly empty once more. Now the band played again, and soon coffee was served.

An eleventh-century scholar, Bachya ibn Pakudah, mused: "Life and death are brothers; they live in the same house. Life is the entrance, death is the exit." Nice words these are, but not necessarily soothing to any of us that are feeling the transition from youth to maturity, confronting and *learning from* the reality that life is not unlimited. Death is an exit that many of us begin to see more often for others, and fear more directly for ourselves. Sooner or later, we discover that being human, we are truly vulnerable to cancer, heart disease, and an assortment of deficiencies and viruses. Mortality is the condition that we were born with, but that went essentially unheeded until this season of our lives. From death, we learn that life ends; from mortality, we learn that life teaches.

This is not a book about death from the point of view of dying, grieving, consoling, and healing; noble and necessary themes that have been well examined by many discerning writers and thinkers, ancient and recent. This is a book about coming to terms with mortality itself, which is the litmus paper of life.

Almost every book I pick up about people and mortality begins with pretty much the same sentence: "Life and death are part of the same cycle." Well, that's true, but it's not clear where that leaves us on any given day of this life. When a middle-aged man, in reasonably good health, comes and tells me that he's afraid of dying, and that he wakes up at night shivering in fear from the thought of his mortality, I'm not sure how meaningful it is to remind him about the cycle of life. The man has a high-profile position, is a good father to three children, and enjoys a peaceful marriage. But, suddenly, he's at the same age at which his father suffered a debilitating heart attack, and up till now, he has not given too much serious thought to the facts of his finitude.

When a young mother calls me on the telephone to describe her slow recovery from ovarian surgery, I hear in her voice the call of the generations. "My mother had this operation when I was a kid!" She complains with a mixture of awe and anxiety. "Who would have thought that, at thirty-eight years old, I'd be laid up like this? And it hurts a lot, too! I guess the years are just starting to creep up on me."

The years don't actually creep up, they just happen. I look at my own two daughters, now in their teens, and recall how skeptical I was, even resentful, when people commented to me years ago: "Wait! It goes by so fast. And then your little girls are suddenly all grown up, and you are thinking about their love lives, their colleges, their engagements. Just wait and see. It'll all happen before you even know it."

It has happened, just as my friends predicted. My babies have filled out, achieved in school, been hurt by insensitive boys, cried transition tears, and watched me grow grayer, thicker, and slower. They have stood by the open graves of some of their relatives— people who were once quick and knowing giants to me and to my wife. I hear my daughter on the telephone, describing the woman whom I remember as my young and vibrant mother: "We're going to go visit my grandmother."

My daughters have seen me in moments of doubt about my professional skills, my ability to hold other people's interest, my health. They tremble at the thought of my vulnerability; they have compassionately sat through my dissertations about my own father, who died before they were born. "I wish you had known him," I'll say to them, often unconsciously adding strands of legends to the facts of his life. My daughters—astute, knowledgeable, relatively patient— probably sense that when I tell them about their departed grandfather, I'm also yearning to reveal myself.

Nevertheless, now it's me, and not my father, who leads the holiday dinners around the table; it's my wife and I, and not our parents, who lie awake at night worrying about the finances; it's our children, and not us, who will be in college at the turn of a century my wife and I and our friends once thought was as far away as the sky.

The seasons change. When I look at the celebrity magazines my daughters bring home, I see glamorous and athletic figures with unimaginable salaries who were born in the 1970s or even later. These are people who wield power and who came into the world *after* my generation buried the Kennedy brothers, Dr. King, and so many youngsters who perished in Vietnam. Suddenly, inexplicably, what was fresh and urgent and frightening and scandalous for me and my generation is dry history for my daughters and their peers. Meanwhile, although I am blessed with fine health, my feet hurt more than they used to, I'm taking before and after antacids, I have my blood pressure routinely measured whenever I see the doctor for even a sinus infection, I take an aspirin almost every day because it's supposed to protect me, I get tired in the afternoon, I get irritated when somebody who just turned twenty-seven complains about growing old, and I contemplate a cemetery with more respect than ever. I am raising my children, nurturing my marriage, burying my kin, confessing my mortality.

The biblical Psalmist wrote: "What person shall live and not see death?" But I understand more than the simple notion that life and death are part of the same rhythm. I understand that the universe is

in motion *because* my father died; *because* my mother who once comforted me is older and depends upon her children; *because* my wife's
parents both grew infirm and couldn't always remember dates; *because*
my sister-in-law who once raised a ruckus at Berkeley is suddenly
over fifty, twice divorced, and uncertain; *because* the youthful woman
who cuts my hair doesn't know any particular grief over the loss of
John Lennon. I accept that the world is rotating *because* I'm the one
paying income taxes, *because* I'm the one whose estate will protect my
children, and *because* the congregation that I serve has an insurance
policy to safeguard it if I should suddenly die.

Mortality should make us think. Some serious, clarifying questions arise: Against the reality of life's limits, and in view of its preciousness, just how much is enough money? Am I as satisfied, truly
satisfied, as I am prosperous? How consequential to me is acclaim or
power? Am I gaining as much wisdom as stress from my job? Would
disloyalty to my life's partner really accomplish something worthwhile for me? Is my ego serving me well, or am I serving *it* in blasts
of vanity and self-importance? How worthy is my criticism of my
youngster regarding her grades or clothing or weight? Do I share as
many values with my family as I do valuables? Am I developing a
meaningful legacy for people who will one day remember me?

In short, mortality causes us to ask: *What is important?*

In the course of my pastoral work, I have seen that a thoughtful
acceptance of life's limits can create a personal feeling of well-being.
A little bit of prayer can be more helpful than a lot of portfolios.
Death need not be feared and it cannot be evaded in acts of out-
rage, impropriety, or narcissism. Meanwhile, often enough there is
relief in death, serenity in death, gratitude in death, even blessing in
death. I have seen this in people who regarded and practiced life
with a measure of sanctity and thankfulness. When people die, the
way they pass on tends to reflect the way they lived. Folks I knew
who were sweet to life generally died sweetly; those who had something to do with God generally went into "the cool night" without a
lot of fanfare; those who were hard on themselves struggled propor-
tionately in their deathbed.

In the course of many years of work with the living and the dying,

I have come to regard mortality with respect and reverence, acknowledging its magnificent tyranny as the sure sign that there is some kind of greater hand that guides the universe.

Meanwhile, mortality also means vulnerability—to illness, bad luck, accident, violence, and an assortment of other circumstances. I don't think I fully grasped the mercurial nature of mortality until my friend Jack Bluestein vanished without a proper good-bye from me.

Jack was my classmate and cohort in graduate school; we studied together to become rabbis. Heavy-shouldered, overachieving, and wickedly funny, Jack had played football in college, married too young, and, as it turned out, chose the rabbinate because he sought to become the first Jewish televangelist. I actually never quite accepted Jack's rather self-serving view of the clergy, and his clamorous personal habits sometimes made me nervous, but I recognized immense talent in him. We were inseparable during those formative years, studying for exams together through the nights, playing pranks on our classmates during the days, fielding a school softball club together, devouring life at a time when it seemed as eternal as it was demanding. My friend was ravenous—for recognition, for sexual gratification, for late-night burgers, for a piece of the sky. Although I knew of his vanity, I was constantly drawn to him for his insightful and devastating humor, his ability to win people over, and his utter brilliance.

When, years later, I suddenly found myself watching Jack Bluestein on CNN's *Larry King Live* discussing his new-wave, big-tent Jewish "revival," I knew that my friend was in the full throttle of his robust ambition. I laughed out loud, recalling the time he had literally placed rubber-tipped toothpicks in his eyes and told me that he was going to be up all night to study for a Talmud exam.

What I did not know when I discovered Jack on national television was that he was already an advanced leukemia patient. After graduating together, he had gone down to Florida to start a congregation, and I went to Canada for my first posting. Freed of academic pressures, we did not need each other in the same way. He would call me once in a while, make me laugh, and then go out and get himself some more air time somewhere. His tenuous marriage finally foundered. But, as it turns out, he was sick; his mighty torso was weakening from poor blood counts, marrow transplants, and chemotherapy. He mentioned his ailment to me from time to time but I refused to imagine him as anything but hale and boisterous.

I had seen Jack during a visit to Florida just prior to the diagnosis. It had been a good sojourn; he confided things to me about his professional goals, his love life, and his disdain for organized religion. The other rabbis in his community shunned and disliked him. Although his lifestyle made me uncomfortable, I found a strange bit of truth in his vision of Judaism without walls, and thought that he was the one who could and should pursue it.

All in all, however, I gave Jack only a cursory thought from time to time. I went on with my career and basically lost track of him— until the Larry King appearance. We saw each other one more time after that, during a rabbinical convention. He told me that he was going to overcome "this cancer thing" and still had big plans. "My congregation renewed my contract," he declared, sounding like a veteran football player who had been given a sentimental extension. He looked small, nervous, lonely. It occurred to me that somebody like Jack could actually die. I didn't think that somebody like *me* could die; but that maybe Jack could.

He called my office, now in Cleveland, many months later. My secretary told me that he was funny, but really sounded troubled. "He wants to talk to you." I wrote myself a note to call Jack sometime.

The note was still in a file in my desk when the newsletter published by our rabbinical conference arrived three weeks later. As everybody who gets such a professional newsletter invariably does, I turned almost immediately to the personal items. There, under the obituary announcements, I read the name JACK BLUESTEIN. In panic and shock, I looked at the name again, rubbing my eyes. I checked the other three names in that month's column. Their life spans made sense: seventy-nine years old, eighty-two years old, ninety-one years old. Under Jack's name, the announcement read "1950–1990," and "Survived by his Parents and Children."

Tears running down my cheeks, I reached into the desk file. I pulled out the note I had made myself just weeks earlier. I stared at the telephone and put my head down in remorse and despair, and I began to tremble.

The next day, I wrote an anguished note to Jack's parents. They surely would remember me; after all, Jack and I had been close buddies, and he had served as an usher at my wedding. I recalled that when my father died just months after my wedding, Jack didn't leave my side for days. "I can hear Jack's laughter right now," I wrote to his mom and dad. I never received a reply from the parents of my friend.

Jack was not a saint. I'm not even certain that he was a perfect father or an effective rabbi. But Jack was mortal, and this is where I neglected him shamefully. His death, bereft of my good-bye or even my acknowledgment, has fueled my intention to regard human life and human mortality with a reverence equal to the emptiness I knew the day I read his name in somebody else's journal.

I have been informed by my work and experience with the living and the dying. This book derives from my seasoning with the life cycle. My own innocence about mortality has been left behind in the soil and mud of countless cemetery walks, the echoes of hundreds of eulogies, the refrain of limitless prayers spoken, chanted, or whispered by crypts, at bedsides, in homes, in hospitals, or in the open air. Mortality leavens human vanity, humbles every soul, and levels all indulgence. It teaches us patience, enlightens us with perspective, blesses us with wisdom.

This is certainly a book about death. It is about people saying good-bye, dying well or not so well, leaving various legacies behind. In this book, we shall also visit with people who confront death in their daily lives, including doctors, reporters, clergy, funeral directors, police officers. This book will also relate the story of one exemplary life—that of a woman named Emma Bennett who mastered her own mortality and taught others to do the same.

Mortality is shared by everybody, but its impact upon each one of us is singular, paramount, and enlightening. This book is not about how we die, but about how we can and should live *because* we die.

Chapter One

What Does Dying
Teach About Living?

In the Book of Exodus, a group of Hebrew elders is allowed to briefly see God. It happens in the twenty-fourth chapter, as Moses escorts this exclusive committee of leaders to their glimpse of the Almighty atop Mount Sinai. It's an unusual episode in the Hebrew scripture, where only Moses is understood to communicate with the deity face-to-face. One wonders what the biblical author had in mind with such a curious story; it is somewhat out of character for this literature in which men and women are understood to perceive and converse with God, but only through dreams or trances or third-party reports. After all, as it says in Deuteronomy, "the secret things belong to God."

But here in Exodus, God evidently decides to open heaven's door just a bit wider than usual: "Then went up . . . seventy of the elders of Israel, and they saw the God of Israel." A few scant details are even included just to tantalize us: "And there was under his feet the like of a paved work of sapphire stone, and the like of the very heaven for clearness." Reading this account, one understandably yearns for some exclusive information, some intelligence on the dynamics of divinity. Maybe the elders will ask some questions while they are tarrying.

Alas, there is nothing hard here, nor even metaphysical. Any potential inquiries about how and why life and death work are quickly squashed by the immediately ensuing biblical verse: "On the

nobles of the children of Israel God did not put his hand." We are
left only with a terse, meager, and equivocal statement: "They saw
God, and they ate and they drank." What did they possibly eat?
What did they drink? We don't know very much about the whole
thing, except that they left, apparently nourished, certainly dazzled,
probably puzzled, definitely mortal.

I think that this little diversion in Exodus is a metaphor for our
relationship with mortality. We don't really know very much about
the enterprise of eternity. We may certainly imagine the face of
heaven, but at the end of the day we are basically left with what we
"eat and drink." We depend upon our own knowledge, our creativity,
and a little bit of faith to help us deal with such things as phantom
sapphire stones, fanciful astral banquets, and why we die.

Even Moses, who supposedly chatted with God, was mortal. In
fact, he died without ever achieving his dearest personal goal—to
get to the Promised Land. But Moses's death served a purpose:
Someone younger had to assume the mantle of leadership. Joshua,
the successor, wasn't as jaded by so many years of difficult responsibility. Joshua hadn't confronted the demons of Egypt or borne the
lonely rigors of administering the freedom walk. He was fresh, without too much cynicism. This kind of situation, bittersweet, poignant,
inevitable, is observed sooner or later in most every corporate board-
room, professional institution, military installation, movie studio,
college administration, church, or synagogue hierarchy. Maybe we
die to make room for the progression of ideas.

In *Gates of Repentance*, a prayerbook published by the Central Conference of American Rabbis, it is written:

> If some messenger were to come to us with the offer that death
> should be overthrown, but with the one inseparable condition
> that birth should also cease; if the existing generation were given
> the chance to live forever, but on the clear understanding that
> never again would there be a child, or a youth, or first love, never
> again new persons with new hopes, new ideas, new achievements;
> ourselves for always and never any others—could the answer be in
> doubt?

I remembered this devotion when visiting with Emanuel Forsch, Jr. Emanuel was ninety-four years old, in hospice at home, dependent upon oxygen, and quite impatient. When I entered his bedroom, he was sitting up in a wheelchair wrapped in a blanket, and eager to converse. His two daughters, Betty and Carla, sat on the adjacent bed. They kept their moist eyes on their father. "How are things with you, Emanuel?" I inquired.

"Rabbi, I am here to die." Betty and Carla smiled. They were familiar with their father's directness, and were grateful for his apparent harmony with the situation. I also noted Emanuel's frankness with a certain amusement. Having had the experience, too often, of burying much younger people—including children—I thought to myself that Emanuel's attitude was commendable. He seemed to understand that ninety-four years of life was quite a gift, even at the close of the twentieth century.

"It's good to hear you declare your readiness to die, Emanuel," I replied. "Now we can talk together straight to each other, particularly with your daughters in the room."

"That's fine," barked the old man. He looked at his two grown-up children, and then spoke to me: "They don't understand how lucky I've been. I'm not sure I deserved to live this long. And I was doing everything I wanted to until just a few weeks ago. Why do you suppose I'm still around?"

"I guess God isn't too angry with you, Emanuel. You have been given long life."

"Well, it isn't all that it's cracked up to be."

"What do you mean?" I was quite curious, and wanted to get some insight from someone who had clearly outlived his own bargain with mortality.

"I mean I did everything I wanted to do and whenever I felt like it. Played golf till just a few months ago—"

"We got him to give up the car just three months ago," interrupted Betty. "He was still driving!"

To this, Carla, visibly filled with affection for her cantankerous dad, added: "I'm not sure he still wouldn't be behind the wheel of his Olds if he wasn't hooked up to so many things in here."

"Well, whatever," growled her father. "My point is that, since I got to live for so long and do what I wanted, why can't I just die already like I want?"

The question hung above the cramped, steam-filled bedroom for a moment. I looked at the two sisters but did not detect any special discernment about their father's wish to die sooner than later. They were clearly resigned to his end, which was coming soon. But they did not seem to maintain or share any conspiratorial notions about helping Emanuel to a quicker conclusion. Nor was he making any specific demands or requests—at least not in my presence. So I concluded that this was not a question about euthanasia, it was just a matter of a man who had had enough of life and was simply looking forward to leaving this world at the suitable moment.

"Emanuel," I said, "how do you wish to be remembered?" Betty and Carla appeared to tense up with the question, but they remained silent. The dying man, keenly in touch with his mortality, had set the tone for this encounter. I thought it would be appropriate and meaningful for his daughters to hear his testament.

Emanuel's eyes seemed to be looking down an ethereal lane that only he could visualize. His brow relaxed. His tone was softer as he spoke:

"How do I want to be remembered?" he mused. "Just for having lived for a real purpose," he finally answered, clearing his throat and perhaps much more of himself. Breathing audibly, he turned toward Betty and Carla, who edged closer to him. "*This* is the purpose," he declared, talking to me, but staring at them. His hands trembled a bit. He began to recount his family history. His grandfather had come from Vienna and peddled goods on the road between Allentown, Pennsylvania, and Toledo, Ohio. Emanuel remembered many details about his childhood: His father, stern and distracted with creating a fortune; his mother, ever present and dutiful and forever making beds; the beginnings of a prosperous family furniture business; the close-knit neighborhood on the east side of Cleveland; the vagrant uncle who had embarrassed the family with philandering and poor investments; his departed wife, Marisa, who had set such an elegant table at Passover; his comely yet very different daughters.

Betty was like her mother, he stated. She was refined and soft-spoken. Carla was shrewd at the business, and was independent and outspoken. "You were much more like me, sweety," he told his younger daughter, whose tears came down in a gentle shower of contentment. "But it was good, Betty, that one of you was like your mother, because she made a man out of me that people could stand being around!"

Emanuel laughed out loud at himself, and we all joined in. It felt so good to share in Emanuel's self-mockery. Betty and Carla were considerably at ease now. Their father, though dying, was nonetheless himself. Too often, we treat the dying as though they are no longer living, as if the fact of one's mortality suddenly denies him or her the salient characteristics, attributes, or flaws that defined that person. We sometimes forget the very things that made somebody so familiar when he or she is dying.

If a person sparkled with a sense of humor through life, he wants us to notice and enjoy it all the more so at the edge of his mortality. If somebody normally tended to anger, she will likely be quite angry at the end. When somebody is dying, he or she is the same person, only more so. We send them to an even greater loneliness when we act as though they are altered people exactly when they are trying to define themselves for our memory.

The tenderness of this moment involving Emanuel and his daughters was exactly as it should have been. He was not a particularly effusive man, nor necessarily a totally agreeable man. But he was intuitive enough to understand that it was necessary for him to die, and that part of his obligation to mortality was to make room for the next generation. Whatever he may have endowed his daughters in some estate document, he was trying to will them now a piece of his heart. Emanuel was quite unafraid, I thought, because he was genuinely reconciled to the cycle of the seasons that is impelled every time a human being is born. He also was cognizant of the gift he had been given of a ripe, old age.

This was evident in the next phase of his deathbed soliloquy, when Emanuel recalled his long-lost friend Peter.

Emanuel had drifted off for a moment or two, but the comfort level achieved in the narrow hospice chamber made his brief silence a natural part of the dialogue. And then he was saying: "Peter was such a patriotic fool!"

I looked at Carla and Betty, who exchanged knowing glances. Carla, her eyes twinkling, began to explain: "Peter was his boyhood friend—"

"I can speak for myself! I'm not dead yet," snapped the old man. "It just doesn't make any sense, Rabbi," he continued as he turned his head toward me.

"What doesn't make sense, Emanuel?" I was concerned that the emotional equilibrium of the room might be threatened by something. "Do you want to tell me about Peter?"

"Peter was born exactly one week after me," said Emanuel. He was highly focused for the moment, his brow a map of the past. "We were both eighteen years old when the Americans started going over for the war."

"You mean World War I?"

"No, the Civil War." Emanuel was rolling his eyes. "Just figure it out, Rabbi." His tone was impetuous but not sarcastic. I genuinely liked him, and was fascinated by the potential for a glimpse into living history.

"Well, Emanuel, go on. Please tell me about Peter. Did you both go over in 1917?" I saw a developing sadness in the daughters' eyes; Carla looked down at the wooden floor.

"We did everything together," Emanuel continued. "Peter was left-handed, and I'm a righty. He didn't want to have anything to do with religion or prayers. I mean, he wasn't an atheist or anything. But I liked to say our prayers, and I memorized the twenty-third psalm, like we were supposed to at temple. Do you know the twenty-third psalm, Rabbi?"

"I think I've heard it before, Emanuel," I replied, feeling a bit impetuous myself. Nonetheless, he began to recite it.

"The Lord is my shepherd, I shall not want. He maketh me to lie down in green pastures; He leadeth me beside the still waters . . ."

He shut and opened his eyes. In a whisper, he repeated the

phrase: *"Beside the still waters."* Then his voice trailed off. He was with Peter again, romping under the high trees along 105th Street in central Cleveland. Sunshine danced through the treetops as the two boys raced along a familiar pathway, breaking twigs and crunching dry leaves under their hard saddle shoes. The trolley struggled along nearby Euclid Avenue, and Emanuel and Peter eventually ran alongside, catching it near 96th Street. They were both fourteen years old, and their mission was to get some dark, pecan chocolate at the Arcade downtown. The wind blew up from Lake Erie, just a mile or so north of the trolley line. Peter and Emanuel looked up and saw waterspouts in the otherwise crystal-clear sky. Emanuel loved it when the clouds, the wind, and the water joined forces in this fashion. *"Look, Peter, the spouts. You see, that's God making things happen in the heaven."*

"It's not God, Manny. It's just the way of the world. Music is heaven, stupid. And beautiful paintings that we see at the museum. And Elisabeth Frankel's body when she wears that pink dress."

Now, sitting next to his deathbed eight decades later, Emanuel came back to me and his daughters. "Only Peter called me Manny. Well, sometimes my mother did, but I loved it when Peter did. Nobody has ever called me that since then, and nobody ever should. Use Emanuel at my funeral, Rabbi."

"I certainly will, Emanuel. Do you want to recite more of the twenty-third psalm? Maybe we'll join you."

The old man looked at me blankly. He was in spiritual pain, and it troubled me deeply. Carla and Betty had never met Peter, but they knew him intimately. Looking suddenly smaller under his wraps, Emanuel was a latticework of memory, morphine, and the murmur of a boy calling "Manny!"

"He restoreth my soul. He guideth me in straight paths for His name's sake. Yea, though I walk through the valley of the shadow of death, I will fear no evil, for Thou art with me; Thy rod and Thy staff comfort me."

The other three of us had joined in by now, reciting the old poem. Emanuel's eyes were filled with tears as he looked up at the ceiling and asked: "Why did you think you had to go over to France to die a good death, Peter?"

"Daddy, don't torment yourself now again," cried Betty, who put both of her hands in her father's trembling, pale, bony palms. Carla sniffed in her tears, then drew a long breath. She whispered, simply, "Daddy." They were both accomplished women in their sixties, slender, charming, well adjusted, intelligent. Both had adult children; Betty had two grandchildren. Yet, in this transition, mortality exposed, Betty and Carla were just two daughters surrendering their father. No matter how old we or our parents are, when we lose them, they are still, simply, our mother and father.

"Emanuel," I said now, "tell me about Peter. What do you mean that he went over to France to die a good death?"

"Peter didn't like all that was happening in the city," responded the old man. "He thought that skyscraper downtown was something vulgar. It was Babel all over again, he said. He hated the obsession people were having when we were kids with the automobile, and all the new mechanical inventions. God, he would have hated computers!" Emanuel laughed to himself, swallowing a bittersweet inhalation of oxygen. "Peter loved the gardens in our neighborhood, art, music. He thought America had lost its soul by being cut off from Europe. Can you imagine? We were just boys, and he had all that in him. So then the war came. At first he despised it, naturally. We heard about the big, new guns, and the killing machines on tracks, and we heard about mustard gas and all that. I thought it was all a million miles away from us." Emanuel paused to gain a little strength. I sensed that his daughters wanted to tell me the story, but they understood that it was very important for their father to tell it himself.

"Then, well, he started to get some new ideas. I thought he was just being his fanciful self at first. You mentioned 1917. That's the year. A very bad year. They started inducting boys into the service to send them over and help the Europeans finish their damn war. Get the Kaiser. But Peter . . . Peter, who I thought couldn't hurt a fly, who was always humming waltzes, Peter signs up with the army! And do you know why? He wanted to do something for France! Can you imagine? He got caught up in this notion—and he wasn't the only one—that he could go over there, to his beautiful France, and save world culture! So he did, all right. Peter. He was killed the very first week—died on his holy soil. We were just boys, and he felt so much that I didn't really understand."

I was shaken by the realization that Emanuel was still grieving for a friend who had died in war almost eighty years prior. Looking at him, I understood that the wound was as old as the twentieth century, and as new as when he opened his eyes that same morning.

"Emanuel," I asked him now, "do you feel guilty that Peter died and you lived?"

"No, I don't. Well, I did for a while. But what I can't accept is that he died for some notion of art and culture. Peter loved cathedrals, and he had this idea, this obsession, yes, that he had to go over to this land of grace and defend the cathedrals! A boy from Ohio doesn't die for France. You die for your children. You die for your grandchildren, like I'm doing. You die to give somebody else something. I don't mind dying. I'm ready to die. I've just missed that boy all these years. He should have gotten old, like I did—although this is too old! Peter died for France but I'm dying for my family. You understand?"

I looked at Betty and Carla, who smiled through the tears on their faces. I envied Emanuel, and felt glad for his household. They were sharing fully in his spiritual coda. I said something to Emanuel about the sanctity of friendship, and how Peter surely didn't die in vain. I expressed the idea that their boyhood bond gave Peter the moral framework for his decision to risk his life, regardless of his tender age. I believed in what I was saying, but realized that Emanuel was neither interested nor moved. He was preoccupied with his loneliness for his lost chum, his nostalgia for youth and freedom, his looming death and its meaning for himself and his generations. What I had to say in that room was right, but not so right for Emanuel at that particular moment.

The room again fell quiet, except for the ventilator that operated without soul or mind. An old and important story hung in the warmth. Peter floated away and Emanuel shut his eyes. His lips moved and he finished his prayer: *"Thou preparest a table before me in the presence of*

*mine enemies; Thou has anointed my head with oil; my cup runneth over. Surely
goodness and mercy shall follow me all the days of my life; and I shall dwell in the
house of the Lord forever. . . .*

"Goodbye, Peter. This is Manny."

A few minutes passed. I started to get up. Emanuel gasped, seemingly startled. "Well, sir," I announced, "I'll see you again soon."

"I hope not. I hope I'm dead!" Emanuel's eyes were ablaze with spirit. It would be a little longer, I thought, till God would let this old man go.

"Why can't I live forever?" Natalie demanded of me, as I held her hand in the hospital room. She was, I thought, still relatively young at sixty-nine, and she certainly was alert and feisty. "Why do I have to die?" At least she knew that her illness was now terminal; her anger confirmed she'd crossed the crucial threshold of acknowledgment. But Natalie was not yet in the mode of acceptance, and my heart went out to her.

She truly enjoyed life, and had found expression for this delectation in her classroom. She had taught American history to thousands of high school students for more than forty years. "Everything I ever said in that classroom," she once joked with me, "was outdated by the time those kids actually understood it." *Those kids.* She held the phrase on her lips with a certain familiarity. Natalie Bohlander, with her husband, Fred, who had died suddenly several years prior, had two adult sons of their own. One was a state tourism official, and the other taught English in Morocco. But *those kids* were the ones Natalie craved now, in her hospital room, where she was being treated for an losing battle with an unyielding disease, lupus.

"The wolves are coming to get me," she said one day, bitterly denouncing the association of the carnivorous *Canis lupus* with her disease. "Look at my face, and you will see where they've left their marks." There were, in fact, noticeable lesions on Natalie's cheeks, as well as along her fingertips. The skin along her fingernails was thin and flaky from the malady, and a pervasive rash haunted the flesh around her nose. I understood that she was dying.

Natalie had enjoyed several remissions over the years, and taught in the classrooms of the same public school until the age of sixty-five. Medication had helped her intermittently. It was clear that what gave Natalie the ability to overcome fatigue, joint pain, and afflicted blood serum was her great will. The history teacher enjoyed repeating two particular stories to me: The first was about Thomas Jefferson, who so deeply despised his contemporary, Supreme Court Justice John Marshall. "Every morning, when Jefferson got up, he would ask out loud, 'Is John Marshall dead yet?' " Natalie bellowed with the tale. "God, I love that grit of Thomas Jefferson. Yet I feel for Marshall. I'm not dead yet, and I refuse to die!"

Then Natalie would settle back in her bed, breathe out from the pain, and tell me again about Ethan Allen, the Revolutionary War general. "You know," she'd repeat, "they would come and tell him, when he was so sick, that the angels were waiting for him. And do you know what he said? He said, 'They're waiting, are they? Well, God damn them, let them wait!' " And again, the hoarse, bitter laugh would emerge from the tall but feeble woman, shaking the bed frame.

"Why do I have to die?" she asked me one afternoon, a taut resignation lining her puffy face. "I want to talk to more of those kids."

"What if some of those kids came to see you?" I inquired.

"No!" Natalie actually looked frightened. "They can't see me like this. My own sons were uncomfortable being here. My boys wouldn't look at me, not really look at me directly in the face." Now, the schoolteacher's expression changed to an appreciable anger. I didn't know her sons, but was disappointed by her account—as much for their sakes as her own.

"What did you talk about with your sons when they were here?" I asked, setting aside for now the topic of Natalie's students.

"Oh, their careers, their houses, their friends. I think the weather came up, and there was a reference or two to the National Football League." What an alert, intuitive, if indignant woman was this Natalie, I thought.

"What did you want them to talk about?"

"Well, maybe something about their mother, for God's sake. I *am* dying here."

"You tell me that you're not, Natalie. And I truly understand. I mean only respect, and I feel for you and your frustrations. But I need to ask you, with love, did you tell your sons that you needed to talk frankly about your situation? Maybe none of you really faced things head-on, so the conversation drifted to football."

Natalie looked at me impatiently. She said nothing, and then closed her eyes. She folded her arms across her chest; I noticed the rash build-up on her palms. Maybe I had been presumptuous. Her sons' visit, for whatever reason, had been inconclusive, perhaps painful. Members of a family were not being honest with each other about their mortality. I felt a certain disconsolation for Natalie, her sons, her three rarely mentioned grandchildren, her departed husband. There might have been an opportunity for closure, forgiving, or insight squandered here. I would see what I could do—time and circumstances permitting—to help these family members make peace with mortality. Meanwhile, as I ruminated, Natalie suddenly opened her eyes and burst out laughing.

"What?" I asked, startled and relieved.

"My son Jerry, the one who lives in Morocco, remembered something while he was here that my husband once did. Fred took the boys, Jerry and Rick, to Canada one summer. The boys were in high school. I was teaching a summer school course. I think Fred wanted to show them Canada, just in case they eventually had to go up there to avoid the draft. Fred hated the war in Vietnam, and wouldn't tolerate his sons fighting in such a senseless conflict. Well, anyway, he took them up there to go fishing, but he also wanted some of those damned Cuban cigars." Natalie paused, smiling, while wiping away a tear. "You know, he was such an idiot! He takes his sons up to Canada so they can learn about avoiding a war against Communists in Asia, but he also sneaks back into the United States with a package of Cuban cigars." Natalie looked at me for some indication of my feelings.

"It sounds like he knew what he believed in, and what he wanted to smoke."

"It's a good thing you never took one of my classes, Rabbi." Her eyes twinkled. She continued, now quite animated, as the memories of Fred's broad personality and the aroma of burning cigars drifted into the septic hospital room. "Anyway, as they approach the border at Fort Erie—you know, near Buffalo—the boys remind him that the Cuban cigars are illegal. They tell him that he better do something because they're going to be asked what they have by the guard at the border. Rick, the funny one, tells Fred that if he's ever going to run away to Canada to avoid serving in Vietnam, he doesn't want to have a cigar felony on his record already!"

Natalie Bohlander took a long breath. "God, he was silly, that Fred of mine. I loved him so much. I'm sorry you never really knew him. We had a great time. The kids at school used to ask me why I had always had so much energy—you know, for 'an old lady.' To teenagers, somebody who is forty-three years old is a senior citizen, washed up. Well, actually, my kids didn't ever think of me as ever being washed up. I don't know what my sons think, but my school kids stayed with me. The classroom was a wonderful place. But I told them, each time, that I had energy because my life has a purpose. Go find your purpose, I'd say. But you know what? My purpose was life with Fred. So meanwhile, Fred has got these cigars in the car that he can't imagine parting with. Isn't it strange? I can tell you about the entire history of the United States, but I'm stuck on my husband and his Cuban cigars." Natalie looked at me again for some kind of reaction or approval.

"I'm afraid to say anything, Natalie. You might throw me out of your class or something."

"Ha!" She laughed out loud. "Thank you for not putting on airs, like some of the doctors and some of the visitors. Look, I know I'm really sick. I know I'm so damn unlucky, because lupus usually doesn't kill people. But okay, I'm not stupid. I know my situation. I know my sons, too, for God's sake. They act like *they're* not mortal, like time is something that doesn't run out. But don't put on airs with me here. I'm dying, but I'm still alive! I think, I remember, I can still teach you a thing or two about the Articles of Confederation. And I like to laugh. People come in here and act like they're talking to a dead person. I'll be dead for a very long time." Now Natalie Bohlander was addressing the world at large. "While I'm still here, please do not whisper in my presence like I'm some kind of a defunct cow."

"I understand you, Natalie. And it's a pleasure to be with you." I took her hand, and she squeezed mine with great strength. I honestly felt that a venerable persona was before me, a true realization of American values. She just wanted to be herself, to love her husband's memory, to teach ideas and to shape impressionable minds. A generation of youngsters who had heard her, been touched by her, and been admonished by her now had the responsibility of making her death purposeful. Some would, I thought. Not all, but enough to dignify her teachings by carrying on the eloquence. Living and dying are full when, in between, there is knowledge. Who among us doesn't recall a Natalie?

"So," I asked after a decent interval, "what happened with the cigars?"

"Oh, God. The cigars. Well, Fred decides to put them in a brown bag and hide them in a place where the customs official wouldn't look for anything. He pulls over and tucks them somewhere in the engine. Jerk! They're in line now at Buffalo, waiting to be inspected. The customs guy comes over and starts talking to Fred and the boys: Where have you been? What did you buy? Suddenly, the boys start to giggle and Fred starts to feel pretty anxious because the air outside is filling up with the definite aroma of cigars. Fred tries to look innocent, and the customs guy is, thank God, good-natured. The motor is smoking Fred's expensive, illicit Cubans!"

Natalie laughed again, thoroughly relishing the memory. "Well," she continued, "everybody is just looking at one another. Jerry and Rick are, by now, a little bit petrified, pretty angry at their father. Finally, the officer leans into Fred's window and says: 'Sir, I hope they were at least illegal, so I can feel good about the confiscation.' They were allowed to pass. That car smelled like Havanas for several days. I told Fred that the United States government has its ways of eliciting cooperation, even from automobiles."

Natalie Bohlander died several days later. Although I pleaded with her, she did not permit me to bring a delegation of her students to visit in the hospital. Boisterous, brilliant, resilient for so long, she was, ultimately, a private and proud person. In a final conversation with me, held in the presence of her strangely reticent sons, she allowed that she had to die to let history go forward. "I hope somebody heard me," she said. "If I stick around forever, what kid could grow up and teach somebody else?"

I gained the satisfaction of knowing, for certain, that somebody heard Natalie. Her sons remained distant, though devoted to her in the processes of grieving. I did not know exactly why; I saw that she was a fine teacher, but was unable to ascertain that she was as good a mother. But Natalie's pupils, *those kids*, spoke to me about her with enthusiasm and gratitude. One of them recited a few lines of Carl Sandburg's poetry at the memorial service. The young woman, now a student teacher, told me that Carl Sandburg was not only a biographer of Abraham Lincoln, but a remarkable poet as well. Quoting Mrs. Bohlander, the new teacher said: "Sandburg described life without schmaltz, and with heart." The disciple read from Sandburg's "Kisses, Can You Come Back Like Ghosts?"

> Love is a clock and the works wear out. . . .
> Love is a day with night at the end . . .
> And now we will bury it and put it away
> Beautifully and decently, like a clock or a violin,
> Like a summer day near full-time,
> Like any lovely thing brought to the expected end.

We went to the cemetery and buried Natalie next to Fred. The buckeyes swayed in the autumn wind. It was a bit too soon for the snows. When we walked away, I thought I smelled a wisp of cigar smoke, and could have sworn I heard some familiar laughter.

I truly perceived that one generation gives way to another, whether or not we are prepared for it, at the funeral of my wife's Aunt Pauline. I also understood that death is something that happens in the flow of the ages, and, if we're lucky, we can discover much when confronted by it.

My wife, Cathy, grew up surrounded by family. It is something she has always cherished and appreciated; the norm for her was to be in the presence of grandparents, uncles, cousins, and at least one other aunt who actually lived with Cathy, her sisters, and her parents. The funerals were unhappy, but they were expected, and the dead were always people she'd been familiar with. It was just before the era of sanitized death in hospital cubicles and with clinical attachments; Cathy clearly recalls—without too much fanfare—the sight of her Grandfather Joseph dying in front of her in the living room. She remembers her Uncle Elliott's constant silly puns, her Aunt Connie's lively stories, and, in general, the smell of ancestral chicken soup, gefilte fish, and goose liver in her house.

But Aunt Pauline was one of the last. Her husband, Billy, had already passed away; one by one, the faces around the table, some encouraging, others maddening, had disappeared, even as the new generation of children blossomed. Cathy and I were making the mournful trek from Cleveland to Columbus all too often within a few short years. But Pauline, in her seventies, had been so particularly youthful, amusingly extravagant, seemingly immortal—until the cancer quickly came and took her away.

As always, we arrived at Epstein's Memorial Chapel in Columbus for the service. A few of the faces one always sees at funerals, some easily discernible, others only vaguely familiar, were already present in the foyer and chapel. Cathy and I ritualistically made our way to the "family room." Pauline's death had stung; she just didn't seem to have ever grown old enough to die. Nevertheless, these gatherings at Epstein's were strangely fortifying, even as we would draw close to the aunts and uncles who, by their presence, offered a sense of continuity.

We entered the family room. It seemed strangely uncrowded. There were Pauline's children, a few of the other cousins our own age, and a sprinkling of the grandchildren. We looked about, as we always did, for the elders. It was then that we realized, with a sickening start, that they simply weren't there anymore. The room was filled with empty spaces. Pauline was gone, but so was Billy, Connie, Elliott, Bootie, Sadie, Ted, Terry, and so on. Cathy's parents were still there at the time, older, hurting, *looking for us*. But essentially, the generation that nurtured us and protected us had wizened and disappeared. We had not prepared for this unsettling revelation; it found us out at the appropriate time. The curve of mortality was bending low into our previously unassuming lives. That day, I began to realize that we die to make room for others. The spaces that were once filled by the parents were necessarily being filled now by the children. Wisdom comes from recognizing this, even if we children are so naturally reluctant to wise up to it.

"I hadn't ever wanted to be in this room without my parents," said Pauline's daughter, Nina. But we do, all of us, eventually enter that room. I learned from Pauline's funeral that we who are younger parents *have* to grow up and plan for the time when our own parents simply won't be there with their insights, their bolstering, their emotional reinforcement. I learned from that forlorn day to spiritually reinvest my relationships with my surviving elders. I have subsequently guided others not to neglect or take for granted the well-being and presence of parents, grandparents, and other valued ancestors, because there comes a time when we find ourselves suddenly alone.

Too often in my work, I have encountered adult children—good people in their forties or fifties—who for far too long depended upon the physical immediacy of their parents. These middle-generation parents, sandwiched in between children and grandparents, have failed to imagine life without the all-knowing, all-supporting intervention of their aging mothers and fathers. They have thus also failed to grow. The older parents are still paying the bills, delivering sustenance, controlling social habits. It is essentially well intended, but the effect can be that adult children, raising their own children, emerging into their own middle age, are not conditioned to accept the responsibility that their parents' mortality is going to impose.

Without the intuition gained from accepting our parents' vulnerability, we enter life's later years still chained by innocence. I truly believe that a key purpose of death is the emotional disclosure it forces upon life. People I have met who haven't previously dealt with someone's death often mean well. But when it comes to knowing about life, people who have suffered usually mean business.

My wife's cousin, Nina, was ready. She had thought through the fact that her parents were not going to live forever. She honored both of them with her love, her devotion, her stirring eulogy at Pauline's service, and ultimately, her inner preparedness for the "room" in which she found herself.

When a woman in my congregation suffered a seizure at home late one night, she was rushed to the hospital by her husband (himself recovering from a recent bypass operation), her daughter and son-in-law, and two of her grandchildren. The son-in-law, a sweet and devoted man, had an unusual perspective on the situation: He is an anesthesiologist, and is around sick people every day. His mother-in-law recovered quickly, and resumed her active schedule within three days. But the doctor, kind, sentimental, previously untainted, was now a different person. The emergency awoke something in him. Fear and a healthy realization had lined his soul: "They really are going to leave us," he came and told me, his voice choking, his eyes wet with experience. He had been near this kind of situation hundreds of times, he told me. But he had never really been close to any of it—until now, when mortality became a personal, and not a general encountering. I thought that the doctor, already skilled and beneficent, would nonetheless have more to offer to his patients from that day on. Always dutifully attending to his patients, the doctor, husband, and father would now truly be in attendance. A breath of death yields a good swallow of life.

Emma Bennett came a long way to die at her home in Ohio in 1997. Her life's journey, begun in a small Canadian town in 1935, weaving together two religious faiths and several useful careers, was fascinating and edifying. As a child, Emma watched her mother, a teacher, cheer and comfort homesick boys at a small, private college. This was likely a key inspiration for Emma as she observed her mother age and as she made her own life choices. Touched by much misfortune, including the violent death of a nephew and life-threatening injuries to her niece and her own son, Emma turned her experience into enlightenment.

"I have the best of both worlds," Emma often enjoyed saying. On the immediate level, the one-time nurse turned Emmy-winning educational broadcaster was referring to her mutual contact with both doctors and patients. On another level, Emma, who lived so well and then died so nobly, was describing her knowing and prescient relationship with both sides of this life. Emma Bennett, whose lifespan and story will help fill this book, was the master of mortality. She helped others make peace with it; she made peace with it when she herself was dying.

I once asked Emma, a gardener, teacher, and mother, why she knew so much about being human. Smiling, she answered matter-of-factly, paraphrasing Ecclesiastes, "Because there's a time to be born, and a time to die. Until that changes, I'm just going to be one of those humans."

So why must we die? The elders of Israel, whisked off to a banquet with the angels, didn't even ask. Perhaps they knew that the answer was in the very fact of their living.

Chapter Two

Coping with the Fear of Mortality

In his book *A Question of Character*, Thomas C. Reeves wrote the following about John F. Kennedy: "Jack took the loss of his favorite sister terribly hard. For the next several years, haunted by Kick's death and fears about his physical condition, Jack spoke often of death. [One close friend] thought him 'deeply preoccupied by death' and later recalled a fishing trip in which Jack pondered the best ways to die."

Reeves also reported in this book, which seriously questioned the overall depth and integrity of Mr. Kennedy, that following his sister's death in 1949, the future president grew somewhat as a human being: "Some of his male friends thought that Jack's new view of his mortality made him more companionable and interesting."

There is no question about it: Once we have confronted mortality, and come to hold it in awe, we add a layer or even layers of heightened sensitivity to ourselves. The assassination of President Kennedy fourteen years after his sister's death made virtually everyone more cognizant and wary and mindful of mortality. Those of us who remember that November of 1963 will never forget the fear we had—the haunting sense that *no one* is immortal or immune from the limits of human flesh.

Presidents die, as do teachers, parents and friends. If we never saw anybody else die, we wouldn't understand our own finitude. And, as the biblical Proverbs hold: "The fear of eternity is the beginning of knowledge." My friend Kathleen began her journey to wisdom even before her father died; in the aftermath, she feels deepened in her heart, and she swears that her father's cigarette smoke is still occasionally detectable in her mother's home.

"I'm afraid to die," says the slim hairdresser, pulling her mane of light hair back and then cupping her troubled face in her hands.

I am somewhat disarmed by the announcement coming from such an athletic, generally upbeat individual who remains in good spirits all day, while she works magic on her customers' hair. Kathleen, in her forties and recently married, is a sympathetic and appealing woman. She could be characterized as intermittently Catholic, even as she describes the "automatic Hail Marys" that had cursory impact upon her formative years. She enjoys her work, she likes people, she cherishes a good glass of wine with a friend, and she appears to be a remarkably well-adjusted individual with many attributes. I happen to know that a lot of people in the community truly envy Kathleen, remarking on her beauty and sympathetic nature, noting her great love for her husband and his sons, whom she now cheerfully mothers in their reconstructed family. Kathleen afraid of anything? It would seem so unlikely for this woman with the consistently pleasant nature. Kathleen has an eternal, blondish sheen about her, but it turns out that, beneath the surface, she's pretty much like anybody else when it comes to the matter of mortality.

I say to her: "I thought that maybe the recent loss of your father might give you some insight into life and death."

"I know that my dad's passing tells me a lot of things. But I'm still stuck on what I have felt for a very long time. I don't want to die. I'm afraid of it. I don't want to get sick. I don't want to get old and frail. . . ." Her voice trails off, and I begin to understand a little bit of why this nice woman does so well in the beauty business. Clipping hair, realigning looks, dwelling on image, Kathleen would have been the perfect foil for the process of time. But now I understand that she is deeply sensitive and anxious.

"I didn't worry about this in my twenties and thirties," she continues. "I didn't even think about it. Who does? We're so foolish. But now that I'm into my forties, it scares me."

I suggest to Kathleen that living and dying are part of a natural cycle, much like the changing of the seasons. She listens politely, but seems troubled nonetheless. Her face grows taut; she tells me that her real fear is of time. Kathleen dreads the wintry years.

"I don't want to think about getting older. I never thought I would face it, but suddenly it's here. It scares me. Maybe I just don't understand death enough. It would be nice to know where people went."

I'm struck by the simple eloquence of her last statement. Isn't this the sum of all of humankind's apprehensions and fears? Isn't it the essence of why we have scriptures, catechisms, holy disputations, mythologies? *It would be nice to know where people went.* Kathleen speaks here for Sisyphus, the Greek trickster who tried to outwit the death god, Thanatos; for Moses, who yearned for immortality at Mt. Nebo; for Buddha and the possibility of nirvana; for the Navajo chief who took the dying out of the home in order that the spirit would be more free to travel. Sitting with me in a contemporary, chic, restaurant, with music and smoke and human beings drifting by, Kathleen was essentially engaged in the same "dance of death" that was so much a part of the ethos and art of the Middle Ages. The medievals developed a spectacle that evoked their keen fear of death, even as death was inordinately so much a part of medieval existence, what with plagues, wars, famines, and ravages. Yet, the folk drama of death continues today, playing out violently in so many television serials, news programs, and movies, as well as across the paparazzi-driven tabloids that fill so many grocery checkout lanes and gasoline minimart centers.

The dance of death that romps through Kathleen's mind is as old as time, as current as the hairdresser's next birthday, even more vivid than any time in human history. Most of us, from Pharaoh to Kennedy, have feared death; not enough of us have reimagined life as a result. Few of us haven't wondered what Kathleen, recently bereaved, newly aware, suddenly less youthful, wondered out loud: *It would be nice to know where people went.*

"This is the age of man and his triumphs," wrote psychiatrist Charles W. Wahl in an essay entitled *The Fear of Death.* "But there is a glaring exception to this paean of man's conquests, one problem where all his assurance, ingenuity, and wit avail him nothing; an area which stands in bold contrast to the rest of nature which is malleable to his will. Here man, with all his cleverness, is powerless. He may postpone death, he may assuage its physical pains, he may rationalize it away or deny its very existence, but escape it he cannot."

I understand Kathleen's fears, because I am human as she is, and perhaps also because my profession calls me to many such circumstances. I wish for her the calmness and insight that such exposure has given me: I am in service to the life cycle and am advised daily by it. I am privileged to hear and see people react to it, learn from it, grow from it, succumb to it. It must not be a stranger in the midst of our lives; the more you know it, the less you fear it.

Mortality is the common denominator of our experience; it teaches us to understand the meaning of a baby's cry, the sound of a bride's laughter, the groan of a deserted husband, the song of a delighted grandmother, the final breath of a lonely widow, the last sigh of a satisfied patriarch. The fear of it is the passport to a better relationship with what precedes it.

"Don't you get any consolation from the changing of the seasons?" I ask Kathleen again, hoping not to sound too much like a preacher with platitudes.

"I accept my father's death more than I used to, because I guess I do see that his time had simply come. In fact, his own father died a little younger, at fifty-nine. The year my father was fifty-nine, he was weird. Once he got past that, he was okay. And if God grants me seventy-seven years like my father had, I'll be very grateful."

Kathleen then tells me of the difficulty her husband, Gary, has. Gary's father died in his mid-forties, which is now Gary's age, and he fears that he has only a few years left. Gary's brother lived with dread his entire forty-third year, because that was the year their father expired. Kathleen wonders what this kind of generational pressure says about the question of seasons.

"Every life has its own seasons," I tell her. Recalling a tragedy I had handled a few months before, I added: "Look, I buried a little boy who died in a swimming pool. It turns out, at the age of eleven, he was in the winter of his life."

"That's not fair," says the hairdresser, basically rejecting the image.

"It's completely unfair, and inexplicable," I agree. "But it tells me a lot about the value of life. Kids, particularly teenagers, absolutely do not comprehend that life has limits. People our age aren't much better at this, either. But the fact is, people do die at different ages. In some ways, the terms 'young' and 'old' are relative. When I say that a person ought to look at life with the notion of seasons, I'm trying to say that time and circumstance move at their own paces, and we don't always have that much to say about it."

"I guess you and I," says Kathleen with a smile, "are somewhere in late summer."

"Perhaps, I don't know. But I do know that it's not the springtime, and that I know a lot more about things than I did when it was springtime. My awareness of life and death helps me to settle it all in my head and my heart."

"So is there a season after this life?" asks the hairdresser.

"Well, there certainly may be something. We don't have any absolute evidence that there isn't. I do believe that, and I've sensed it from being around death so often, and I know that it helps people who fear dying so much." I ask Kathleen about something she had once reported to me, not long after her father died, as I sat in her coiffuring chair.

"You mean the cigarette smoke? Yeah, you know, Dad always lit up out on the back porch, because Mom hates the smoke. I used to get a strange, reassuring feeling when I'd come home and smell his cigarettes out there. I'd go out there, we'd both be away from everybody else, and we'd just talk and smoke together. Well, just a few days after he died, Mom calls me and tells me that she smells his cigarette smoke in the house. She was absolutely sure."

"Did it frighten her?"

"No." Kathleen laughs her trademark laugh. "I think she was miffed that he was smoking in the house again!"

"Does it scare you?"

"Oh, no. And it's happened again. It makes me feel good. I really believe he's there, telling us it's all right. No, no. It doesn't scare me."

"Maybe it tells you something about where people go. It seems they go somewhere. Maybe it can help you with your own fears, Kathleen."

This, of course, was hardly the first time I heard such a story. People have found great solace and relief in such encounters with their loved ones. We will deal with the question of the afterlife later in this book; I regard it all with an open mind based on some convincing personal experience. Frankly, I was delighted to hear about the cabalistic smoke, and hoped that it truly gave Kathleen some form of reassurance. She missed her father in direct proportion to how much she loved him; why shouldn't she allow her sensation of his presence help to ease her fear of mortality?

Kathleen pulled back her hair again, lit a cigarette, and blew out a cloud of her own smoke. "It's kind of nice to say it out loud." She exhaled some more. "I feel somewhat afraid of death. I don't want to go there." She pronounced all this now as a kind of summation, as though she were examining her consciousness and not just declaring it.

"Well, it wouldn't be normal for you to welcome it, Kathleen. If you weren't apprehensive about it, there would be something peculiar with your outlook. I'd have to wonder how much you value life if you didn't consider things about death."

"Yeah," she continued, "I don't want the vacation to end." She laughed heartily at her metaphor. "You know, whenever I'm away on vacation up in Canada, surrounded by lakes and beauty, I don't want that to end. But it has to."

But it has to. She looked down at the table. Then she looked up at me, an aura of determination about her countenance. Kathleen was gathering in her life force, coating her fear of death with a new perspective on the mountains of Canada, as well as the faces of her household.

"Don't make me into a grandfather!"

I often wish that my own father had been possessed of a keener fear of mortality. As such, his dismay with eternity was misdirected, and ultimately worked in favor of his dying rather than his living. I learned as much from his death as I did from his life. My father often announced that he did not want to become a grandfather. He got his wish, and I am left with the feeling that his dance with death would have been more sure-footed had he not been so obsessed with the inevitable progression of age.

I know that my father apprehended his death. I discovered evidence of this in his journals, which I read some time after his sudden demise—from a massive heart attack—in the spring of 1976. In painful, searching prose, my father inscribed his struggle with himself in the months before his end. A mild heart attack two years before not only failed to help him discern life better, it actually broke his proud and vain spirit. He could not give in to the reality of his vulnerability, dismissing the precaution and care prescribed by his physicians and pleaded for by his anxious family. He had been an award-winning athlete in college; he was a physically strong and virile young man who made something of a name for himself in his adopted America. He seemed, in his agonizing diaries, to both defy and dread his sentence of mortality. On one hand, he complained of the restrictions to his physical activity that his heart condition imposed. On the other hand, he prophesied that he could see himself in a coffin at Cincinnati's Weil Funeral Home. Remembering his handwritten, Hebrew-laced confessions now, I recall what is written in the Talmud: "Youth is a garland of roses; old age a crown of willows." My father, always fragrant with his hallmark aftershave, blooming with immigrant idealism, was like a rose, blending petals with thorns. My father, given to bursts of sentiment, short on patience, never wore a crown of willows.

I wasn't completely surprised by his unceremonious demise. I had dreamed of it so many times during the final, emotionally stormy years of his life. The dead sometimes come to us after this life; my father's crestfallen soul transformed him into a nocturnal visitor with me even while he was still living. I just *knew* he was going to die, and prayed that my bad dreams were merely an expression of how much I loved him and worried about him. Nevertheless, long before my mother and I were called to the Jewish Community Center to discover his husky form lying under a white sheet in the middle of handball court #2, I was already with him at the foot of the spiritual bridge that leads out of this world. I stared at the spectacle, simultaneously shaken and comprehending. Inexplicably, within the horror, my poor father helped me along with my own fears; his mighty and misplaced person was laid out, and I suddenly was very familiar with the predicament of mortality.

If only he had channeled his own fears into a better awareness. Mutinous, erratically contrite, tormented, resentful of growing old, he dropped dead in the health club, fulfilling his own dark clairvoyance, denying the willows their access, opening new vistas of insight for me equal to my ongoing grief over the loss of his presence in my life. Strange that the bluntness of my father's unnecessary and untimely death has given me a sure sense of what is necessary and what is timely in the category of life. No one I know is looking forward to being a grandfather more than me, and no one is more bereaved that my father didn't discern the autumn wisdom that surely heralds such a blessing.

"Don't make me into a grandfather," he declared, not long after I announced my intention to marry Cathy. My parents were still very young at the time of my engagement, not yet in their mid-forties. It was not so easy for my active, robust father to pour this development into his cup of life. He had found my unfolding life cycle somewhat of a danger to his sense of existence. I have heard this refrain several times since—now from my contemporaries, who seem momentarily sullen, even threatened, when the news arrives of their children's marriage plans, or pregnancies.

When my friend Tom, an aspiring politician and a very good family man, heard that his daughter was engaged, he did not receive my congratulations too comfortably. Tom, fiftyish, had some emotional blockage associated with the whole thing. "I'm not sure I'm ready for this," he said. And then my ears were visited by a disturbing echo: "I can't have them make me into a grandfather." Tom did just fine at his daughter's wedding, and he takes great pleasure in her obvious and abiding happiness. But Tom, like so many baby boomers, could have used some palliative care when first confronted with the rather delicate evidence of his own life's span. It's bittersweet—this matter of time and children and milestones. People do not always accept the turning points without some degree of ambivalence.

But who makes whom into anything? If and when my daughters become parents, I won't be "made" into a grandfather. What I will be is lucky. Unlike my dear father, the knowledge of my eventual death causes me not to want to subtract things, but to add things. I *want* to know the sensation of holding a grandchild—not necessarily tomorrow, but when the time comes. What will I really know of the exclusive insight a living ancestor has until I actually am such a person? Unlike a number of men I have heard from, I am prepared for and intrigued with growing old when the time comes. How will I ever truly acquire the peculiar wisdom, the useful skepticism of the elders unless I'm there? Life is too fascinating to dwell upon the physical virtues of youth; I can't run as fast now as I did twenty years ago, but I sure can think better. I *have* to be this old to know the unparalleled adventure of watching my daughters emerge into their womanhood. I know we pay for it with life itself, but how bereft I would be had I not at least begun to know the seasons of sagacity. *Make me into a grandfather*—it only means my short visit on the earth was extended into sapience. I don't fear death; I fear wasting death.

In the movie *Moonstruck*, the downcast but shrewd matriarch played by Olympia Dukakis rhetorically asks a gentleman who seeks her company over dinner: "Why do men cheat on their wives?" She then provides her own succinct answer: "Because they're afraid to die." There is something to this: I am exposed to, and basically understand, the mid-life crises of men and women I meet. In the 1990s, we adults had more toys, more diversions, more rationalizations than at any time in history. The *New York Times* reported, in 1997, about the rising number of awarded foundation grants for research on the topics of death and dying. "Death is finally coming out of the closet," one physician was quoted as saying.

But I'm not so sure that the new seminars on death have been altogether edifying. The end of the millennium remains rampant with narcissism, materialism, unbridled egotism. Most of us are possessed of extensive electronic power, formidable motor engines, automated services, unlimited access, unyielding information. At the same time, age is covered over and rationalized with cosmetics, drugs, fitness regimens, surgery, and a variety of genuine social and medical break-throughs. The notions of limits and boundaries, of death itself, seem more remote than ever.

Meanwhile, in spite of the hospice movement, death and dying become more sanitized, more removed, more a case—as one reporter lamented—of being "sequestered in care units." Our civilization, a decoupage of neon, celluloid, and software, seems more concerned with receding hair and with spreading middles than with declining literacy and advancing restlessness. Though there are serious medical indications involved, it is no wonder that some men and women fall into profound depressions after even the most successful of heart bypass operations. We are not well trained by society to crave, or even welcome, maturity. My father's death, and my exposure so often since then to the victims of various ailments, have alerted me to the fact that we do not fear death creatively and insightfully. Using the magazine and television culture as a mirror, we feign immortality, only to be terrorized by mortality. We live too fast; we die too poorly. As a friend of mine, then in her early thirties, once asked in exasperation: "What is the rush? We're going to get there anyway. I'd like to see something along the way."

What *is* the rush? The strange thing is that we fear death, we wish to put it off, yet we seem self-propelled into time and space by our choice of social habits, and indulgences, and our desire to gain advantage. With regard to family ties, ethnic sensibilities, and pro-fessional goals, we appear interested in "getting in touch." Yet we rarely "get in touch" with mortality. Anyone who is in touch with mortality would also be linking with eternity and would instinctively know that the earth, universe, and life itself are, like gravity, the most deliberate processes in existence and the least affected by hurry, haste, and bustle.

The stars aren't going anywhere, even if you are bucking for your next promotion. As is sung in the New Century Hymnal: *"The moon shines full at God's command, and all the stars obey."* The Earth is going to consume 365 days in order to revolve around the sun, no matter how many secret relationships you are undertaking in an effort to jump-start your own solar pattern. The summer humidity will press against your busy brow, even if you are determined to vent steam about trivia like your son's or daughter's unkempt room. The autumn will give way to winter, even if you think you won't. The only way to appease your fear of death, and perhaps to gain some perspective, and to loosen your soul, is to let the process of eternity unfold, and lean into it.

How do you do that? I have found, often enough, that people who carry some notion of God in their hearts seem to be more at peace with mortality.

It perhaps shouldn't come as a surprise that a pious man would find some quietude while confronting his mortality. But I was struck by the solid and soothing faith displayed by a friend, Father Anthony M. Pilla, as he passed through the crucible of serious heart surgery not too long ago. Serving as spiritual leader of over a million Catholics in northeastern Ohio, Father Pilla is the bishop of the Cleveland diocese. At the time of his quadruple bypass, he was also president of the National Conference of Catholic Bishops. His cardiovascular situation was the subject of great media interest; he was considered a celebrity patient at the Cleveland Clinic, and came and went with security personnel.

But the bishop, immersed in a God concept, thought of himself simply as a man. While humble in temperament before his illness, he was particularly unassuming and private through his highly public medical passage. "It makes me think even more so of my mortality," he said. He told friends that he really put his situation in the hands of God. Knowing Bishop Pilla, and having prayed with him, I was certain of his total and tranquil submission to divine providence in the matter of his surgery. "I just hope it has made me more sensitive to the human condition," said the quiet priest whose words affect a million lives.

Does the bishop fear death? Certainly, and without any guile. But his fear of death is transposed into a serenity with life because he has matched his predicament in eternity to his conviction in God. As such, this priest, and many much less-celebrated people of faith, actually do face their mortality—especially when mortality stares them in the face—with a measure of calmness and a dimension of dignity. People who have some kind of relationship with heaven fear heaven less than those who are strangers to what is beyond their tangible condition. I have seen it a thousand times: Those who were familiar with prayer, whether formal or not, during ordinary times, were much more composed during extraordinary times. They were, in the bishop's phrase, "more sensitive to the human condition" because they understood the human condition all along.

I have wondered if my friend Kathleen, the hairdresser, might have had an easier time coping with her fear of death had the "Hail Mary" devotions of her childhood not been so "automatic." I have certainly seen Jews, not necessarily doctrinal or rigidly pious, die easier deaths just because a synagogue was part of their normal environment. There is equanimity in maintaining a spiritual link with the moons and festivals of any religious calendar. Following the weekly cycle of the Torah, or living in some cadence with Gospel teachings, or knowing the rhythm of the Koran, or aspiring to the Buddhist condition of oneness—whatever the ritual, however the devotion, an affinity with God is a kinship with mortality. It distills time—slowing the rush, softening the fear, calming the soul. Absent any theology, life empties out, and, as Carl Jung wrote: "Restlessness begets meaninglessness, and the lack of meaning in life is a soul-sickness whose full import our age has not as yet begun to comprehend."

When Scott, a columnist and emerging movie writer, suddenly lost his friend Michelle, he declared that his self-absorption and vanity were bent by a new standpoint. Understandably focused on his own divorce settlement, his new house, a book deal, and other pursuits, Scott, seared by mortality, gained some bias. "I think about my difficulties and challenges," he told me, "and invariably, tragically, there is something to put them in perspective."

Michelle had been admitted to the hospital for a CAT scan. She was reported to have had an extremely rare allergic reaction, Scott noted. "It was to the fluid used in the process, or so I've been told," Scott told me in bitter grief. "Always she had a beautiful smile and sparkling bright eyes. Always a kind word. She was clearly a happy, vibrant woman." Then Scott added: "I'm sure members of her family are looking at their crucifixes and wondering as they grieve."

Looking at their crucifixes? I know that Scott was pointing to irony, and that he was invoking the fathomable skepticism of the non-religious when God appears to have failed the ostensibly religious. But I should hope that Michelle's sorrowing relatives *were* looking to their faith values. And not only would I hope that Michelle's family was now clutching crucifixes, but also that the crucifixes had been there before this terrible test. We fear and discover death often enough; why be forced to confront it without any kind of spirituality? A crucifix, genuinely held, is a useful match for a CAT scan gone bad; a Hebrew psalm can line an empty soul; a sincere examination of an Islamic *sura* can serve to quell a crisis. There is something to be said in mortal existence for developing a harmony with angels. What hurts me for Scott, plaintive, churning, introspective, is that, short one more friend, he finds himself with nowhere to alight.

On a muggy June afternoon in 1986, Robert W. Stewart, a physician at the Cleveland Clinic, dictated a letter of appreciation to Emma Bennett, who produced and moderated a local television program on health care. Dr. Stewart, a specialist in thoracic and cardiovascular surgery, had performed a heart transplant on a young man named Richard Rideout. Mr. Rideout, a large, strapping man, was twenty-six years old, generally active, and vital, but had become quite ill from a viral infection. The infection accelerated into cardiomyopathy—a debilitating condition that can lead to a potentially fatal weakening of the heart muscles. It is likely that Richard would have died without the transplant.

Emma Bennett had devoted the season's final installment of her award-winning program, called *Medi-Scene*, to the subject of Rick Rideout's heart transplant. In 1986, such a procedure was still somewhat distinctive; the special medical unit at the renowned Cleveland clinic that performed such transplants was still only two years old. The program detailed the events leading up to, including, and immediately following the transplant.

At the time of the telecast, Emma's health care issues program had been on the air for less than two years. Emma was the station's director of medical programming. A station brochure promoting *Medi-Scene* celebrated Emma's "blend of two important skills: an understanding of medicine developed through years of practical experience, and the ability to communicate that knowledge to the viewer." The publicity indicated that Emma possessed a bachelor's degree in communications and declared that "she's not afraid to roll up her sleeves and go into the operating room to bring back the inside stories."

Emma personally emphasized that her unique program would focus on the history of medicine. In her press release, she declared that she wanted "to tell the stories of how we have leaped from using blood-sucking leeches to heart implants, and from early wheelchairs to the implanting of artificial kneecaps."

The impact of Emma's television program—the zenith of her unusual and successful career as a nurse-turned-broadcaster—was considerable. Beyond the many professional awards it received, the program, riding on Emma's inviting and confident personality, informed and touched thousands of people who might not have otherwise been exposed to sensitive medical issues. In October of 1985 alone, Emma examined congenital hand problems, arthritis, total knee replacements, hemophilia, and testicular cancer. Always the pioneer, Emma also examined and revealed the world's first embryo transplant into a surrogate mother, and chronicled the first in vitro baby born in the state of Ohio. Through the broadcast medium, Emma, a nurse, brought medicine to people and people to medicine. From balloon angioplasty to the AIDS crisis to her own eventual terminal cancer, Emma Bennett was a patient advocate who thought that doctors were for serving and that life is for living.

At the time of the telecast on Rick Rideout's heart transplant, Emma had been Jewish for a little over twenty years. Her life was filled with interesting transitions—from Anglican upbringing to Passover Seders and Chanukah celebrations; from birth in Canada to college in Ohio; from nurse to broadcaster; from caregiver to patient.

"I remember her as a happy and carefree little girl," recalls her distant relative Dorothy Nicholls. Sitting in her snug cottage in northern Ontario, Dorothy sighed with a pleasant memory from a shared childhood with Emma. "She would come skipping up our driveway and my mother used to say, 'Here comes trouble.' " Dorothy told me that Emma still laughed about that just two weeks before dying, in March 1997.

Dorothy, with potter's hands and a good-natured disposition, had been related to Emma through the remarriage of Dorothy's mother to Emma's older brother. They shared many years in Canada, visiting and calling. "In our house in the town of Thorold, there was a light in the kitchen with a big chain switch at the end of it. Well, Emma came over one day, pulled on it, and the whole fixture came crashing down! She just howled about that. God, how she accepted everything in life, little accidents, and then her own terrible illness. She cherished everything, especially her family, and, of course, her china tea set."

The two women spoke on the phone during Emma's final winter. Dorothy was making plans to come down from Canada for a visit in Ohio. "I'll be gone when you return here," Emma said, without hesitation. She laughed about skipping up the driveway so many years before. She remembered the crashing kitchen light, the splendid china tea cups. "It would be so hard for me to call her when she was sick," said Dorothy. "But Emma would just declare, it's no problem, just call. Some people accept everything so well, including death. Emma was just so in tune with her mortality. She just knew all about it."

Chapter Three

=◈◈◈=

Every Soul Takes Its Own Journey

I remember visiting two different people, both hospitalized, during the same afternoon. Their divergent perspectives on their situations taught me something about this life. The first patient, Mr. Goldin, was a normally hardy gentleman, exceptionally fit, in his mid-seventies. Though I had never grown very close to Mr. Goldin, who was given to brusqueness, I admired his vitality and his feistiness. In business, he got things done; on the golf course, he reveled.

Today, however, Mr. Goldin was not reveling. He was in a private hospital room, laid up with an ankle he'd broken on the fairway. He had somehow lost his footing on what should have been a pristine surface, interrupting his game, his mood, and, evidently, his life. Mr. Goldin was in poor spirits.

My visit with him was not very successful nor useful. "Are you going to tell me that this is what God wants?" he growled. "Is this something I am supposed to learn from?" He would have no part of accepting his predicament.

"I just wanted to say hello," I offered, wondering how a man with a lovely, healthy wife, three successful children, several grandchildren, three expensive imported cars, two homes, and several sets of personalized golf clubs could turn a broken ankle into a theological stalemate. Mr. Goldin softened a bit, and I recognized that he was in some pain. He said: "Well, that's fine. But look, this is just unfair. It is just plain cruel. What am I supposed to do now?"

He railed about the injustice of the situation. Why was God testing him in this way? He would probably be unable to play in the upcoming tournament at his Florida condominium complex. The man was in genuine physical discomfort, but his anguish was interminable, his anger about this inconvenience to his business and social calendars beyond repair. He was inconsolable, in spite of the many gifts of his life. His wife entered the room, along with two of his grandchildren. They smiled at him, getting a tad more warmth in return than I had received. There wasn't much I could accomplish but to listen for a while and then respectfully take my leave.

Just afterward, I visited a woman who lay alone in her room. Following the peevish Mr. Goldin, I actually dreaded what I might encounter now from Mrs. Mayerson—a woman with real problems.

Mrs. Mayerson had been immobilized and bedridden for four months. A deterioration of her spinal cord had effectively ended her active life. I understood that there was no hope for her to ever walk again, or even stand up. As I entered her room, she raised her eyes at me and smiled. I recall thinking that I had never before been blessed by such a beneficent face. She smiled, and absolutely reached out to me with her countenance. Though she was completely still, I felt as though she had wrapped her arms around me.

The woman then proceeded to tell me about her great and good fortune. "Do you know how lucky I am, Rabbi?" She repeatedly asked me this. "I have my children who love me, my beautiful grandchildren who sing to me and write me lovely poems. The doctors are marvelous here and the care is so good. I have such a wonderful life. I know I can't move but I am lucky to be alive and to know the people who make my life worth living."

It goes without saying that I benefited from visiting this remarkable grandmother at least as much as she did from seeing me. I was inspired by her, and remain so to this day. Mrs. Mayerson did not ask me why God had done this to her. When she mentioned God, she said that she had God to fall back on when she needed an extra measure of strength and encouragement. "Do you want to pray with me right now?" I asked her. "I just prayed a little earlier," she responded. "I prayed that my family will be okay if I die from all this, because I really am fine. If I die from this, then it means I was given the time first to realize how much there's been to my life."

As I listened to Mrs. Mayerson, I felt a glow in the room, and I certainly felt ashamed for all the times I had lumped small nuisances, petty annoyances, and minor distractions all together as "the problems of life." I then felt a profound and sincere sadness for the fractured Mr. Goldin, who fidgeted impatiently in his more posh room three floors above in the same hospital. As I heard Mrs. Mayerson celebrate her own inner strength and her obvious accord with mortality, I learned more about God and life than from any previous, extended examination of Talmudic text or scriptural selection.

When Mr. Goldin became terminally ill a year later with lymphoma, he was completely unequipped for the situation. Lashing out at his family, and his employees, he refused to relinquish control of his business affairs. He doggedly maintained his lifelong secretiveness about his personal matters. His children were left with a significant lack of input with respect to the family enterprise. It's not that Mr. Goldin did not know what to tell his children, it's just that he would not tell them. Clouding the atmosphere, complicating the grief, restricting the closure, Mr. Goldin's unwillingness to acknowledge life's limits made his final few months on the earth a desolate passage from material wealth into spiritual oblivion.

I would sit by his side during the final weeks of the illness. He was not very talkative. I watched as he used his right hand to press the bedside device that delivered more morphine into his bloodstream. What a lonely hand, I thought. So many palms pressed in elaborate business deals, yet so few occasions when the hand had actually touched anybody. I was mad at myself: I should have at least offered Mr. Goldin a homily on priorities a year earlier when the grumpy retailer lay in bed with only his broken ankle.

I went over to the nursing home where Mrs. Mayerson had since transferred. She was making minute progress with her spine and, quite miraculously, was able to turn her head just a little. I told her about Mr. Goldin, that he was going to die, and that I felt that I hadn't done enough to enlighten him when he was still healthy.

The rabbinic tradition describes insightful people as "the broken vessels" of life. The tradition actually implies that God is particularly interested in the wisdom of people who have endured something, who have suffered, whose vessels have been, at some time, shattered with experience. I remembered this now when Mrs. Mayerson asked me: "Did he learn anything when he broke his ankle playing golf?"

"No, not really," I answered.

"So what could he learn from cancer?"

I nodded in understanding. Mrs. Mayerson's eyes twinkled, and then she shut them for a nap. People live a certain way, they pretty much die that way, I thought to myself. Unless they become broken vessels. Maybe Mr. Goldin's problem was that, save for a few minor financial setbacks, and a minor mishap between the greens, he never really faced any obstacles.

There are different ways to live and different ways to die. Mr. Goldin is gone; Mrs. Mayerson lives on. He died without seasoning; she exists seasoned by mortality. He had a portfolio of typed invoices; she keeps a file of crayoned poetry from her grandchildren. Meanwhile, in the breadth of one recent summer, three people finished out their lives in three very dissimilar circumstances and at three distinct ages.

Michael London was eleven years old when his family set out for Israel with me. June is so often a month of milestones and journeys; Michael, his older brother Stephen, his younger sister Eliana, his parents, and grandmother joined with forty other people on an annual congregational "pilgrimage" to the Holy Land. Michael's father, Alan, a physician, brought his curiosity and camera along on this special journey that would include—during the course of one day—the bar mitzvah ceremony of one son and the death of the other. Michael's mother, Patty, was of Mexican descent, with smooth skin and a soft voice. She would find her chosen faith of Judaism both exalted in celebration and tested in suffering while in the land of her life's religions.

The milestone day, a Monday, had begun very early in Jerusalem. We had all seen something of Michael's emerging character while having spent the weekend praying, singing, and exploring in the holy city. Michael had been unable to resist handing over some *shekels* to a beggared Arab woman in the walled city that morning. He then was unable to gulp down the exotic Israeli food that we all shared at a banquet that evening, choosing instead—to the consternation of those of us supervising the trip—to exit out the restaurant door and wander about the nearby street with a couple of other young members of our pilgrimage. Inquisitive, indomitable, comely, Michael was a classic, bright child of the suburbs, with an evident love for G.I. Joe action figures.

On that Monday morning after we departed Jerusalem with the dawn, Michael watched while his brother Stephen became a bar mitzvah atop the famous southern mountain called Masada. I blessed five children in this manner on that high and historic spot. There was a splendid clarity to everything that would be shattered just thirteen hours later in the desert night.

At a kibbutz a few hours down the desert road from Mt. Masada, the pilgrims, relaxed, fulfilled, sunburned, sat poolside on Monday night. As most of the group's children cavorted in the water, we felt the gratification of what had been a sanctified day. Just before frolicking at the pool, we had lit candles, sung folk songs, and consecrated one another in the kibbutz synagogue. Alan and Patty London had blessed Stephen while keeping their arms around their other children, Eliana and Michael.

A zephyr came across the arid plain from the Jordanian mountains just east of the kibbutz, lulling and delighting us. The children were laughing and splashing, and, suddenly, somebody realized that Michael was floating on the surface at a terrible angle, his face mostly submerged. Within moments, Masada crumbled, the wind frosted, bringing our laughter and chanting to a stop.

As Michael, now laid out on the poolside pavement, failed to respond to the initial, frantic efforts of lifeguards, doctors, nurses, and his courageous parents, members of our group convulsed and shrieked. We became a frightened, desperate, helpless circle of tears—clutching our children, seeking somehow to shield, console, explain, deny, accept. Strangely serene, Michael lay oblivious to tubes, heart massages, exhortations, CPR efforts, his father's attempts to stroke his little feet and push the life back into his smooth but flat chest. Michael's eyes were open, but his body was closed. I thought I heard a guttural groan emerging from somewhere in the purple desert night; I know my hands were writhing in prayer, foreboding, and mounting responsibility.

We all did what we had to do. We acted on professional instinct, trying to maintain the situation while our hearts were shattering. The group was mostly dispatched back to the synagogue, a medical team was alerted from a nearby army base, grief counselors and psychologists somehow appeared from out of the wilderness night. The heaven above, glowing with starshine yet drooped over the sandy basin, seemed less remote now than civilization. The port city of Eilat was some twenty-five miles away. We were dreadfully separated from what seemed normal.

One of the many bittersweet ironies of this tragedy was that Michael, a little boy who adored G.I. Joe models, was surrounded by such figures in his final moments. Already drifting toward the heaven, Michael was flanked and accompanied by Israeli army doctors—Hebrew G.I. Joes—who had flown in by helicopter and who failed to revive him in spite of their epic efforts and their reluctance to give up on the little boy.

I heard and understood the olive-clad soldiers talking and barking and gasping while faced with the situation. Michael's father would turn to me at regular intervals during the horrifying ordeal, demanding to know: *"What are they saying?!"* Although my Hebrew language skills are good, I did not comprehend all the medical terms the soldier doctors were using, but I knew more than enough of their language of despair. "They're concerned," I said to the poor father over and over again. "The heartbeat is okay, but they don't know why Michael isn't responding. . . ."

Although Patty, the mother, had also attempted to revive her son, she eventually sat by in a lounge chair, beyond the throng of medical people. I went over to her from time to time. She seemed to know, from the outset of the emergency, that her little boy was doomed. Another, younger woman, a member of the ill-starred kibbutz community that had welcomed us, came by regularly and moistened all of our lips with a cool, moist sponge. It was true: We were all, including the stricken mother, growing dehydrated, losing our fluids, our minds, our grasps, our little lad who was turning purple from the well-meaning and futile pounding inflicted by soldiers who were losing this battle by the pool.

I took Patty's hands as she sat, with the uncomprehending Stephen and Eliana on either side of her, and looked into her eyes. "It's just not right," she barely whispered, "for a parent to lose a child." She knew. Her womb was turning inside out, and she knew. She was journeying from this night, via her chosen Judaism, back to her Christian roots in Mexico, and then returning again to this apocalyptic moment in the Hebrew desert that now claimed her middle child. I prayed to myself that every faith she possibly knew or recalled might add its sacraments.

It was well past midnight when the military doctors prepared to depart the scene. The pilgrimage group, changed forever, in shock, huddled within family units, had since retreated to a sleepless night in their assigned kibbutz guest houses. We had just climbed the mountain that morning; now we were in the deepest of biblical valleys.

Patty and her two children, along with Alan's mother—a hopelessly bereaved grandmother—now regrouped at the poolside in order to say good-bye to Michael's lifeless body. There was a discernible stillness in the desert. I stood with Alan and Patty as they exchanged farewells with the sympathetic if businesslike military commander who had supervised the medical team.

Some documents were signed; Michael's passport was requested. The doctor, hardened but not so hard that his face wasn't wrinkled with remorse and sympathy, extended his hand to Alan. The father, destroyed, bewildered, woeful, seemed to understand *the doctor's* anguish. Indeed, from the moment of his son's inexplicably tragic death, Alan London displayed an uncanny and remarkable concern for the feelings of others—especially the children—regarding Michael. Now, the military doctor, an Israeli officer, and the bereft father, a suburban American professional, embraced awkwardly but genuinely. There was no way under the deep, knowing sky of that night that these two men would not somehow cling to each other for an instant. Familiar strangers, they met each other directly on the bridge of mortality.

The nocturnal nightmare gave way to a grim morning. I made dreadful telephone calls back to the United States, trying to ignite a series of events and interventions that would help the mournful family make their way back home with their dead. Alan London, momentarily a dry well of tears, bravely telephoned some of his stateside relatives at dawn, telling them what happened to his middle child. He had to repeat himself constantly; there was always an initial lack of comprehension at the other end of the line.

There were questions about exactly what happened to Michael, even as the coroner in Tel Aviv officially proclaimed a drowning. But Michael's family, particularly his father, were not so sure. Was it a problem with his vagus nerve that caused him to black out while in the water? I would learn that this long cranial nerve, arising in the brain base and extending to the chest, helps regulate the heart rate, breathing, and other functions. Alan London, analytical even in his shock and terror, mentioned that Michael had experienced one or two episodes of losing consciousness earlier in his life. Naturally, the questions swirled, but the one answer that was returned without a doubt was that a sweet little boy who had blessed his brother in the morning had now died in the night. Ultimately, it was determined that Michael died from long QT syndrome, an inherited heart rhythm disorder.

We ate a desolate breakfast together in the kibbutz dining hall while the London family prepared to leave the group. We would all be joined together several days later back in Cleveland, at Michael's funeral. We made the decision to conclude our journey through the Holy Land, even as we dedicated the remaining few days to an important memory. Under the revealing sunlight, the Londons left the kibbutz in a car, heading for an altered life. The rest of us boarded our bus and rode in absolute silence to the city of Eilat. We were received there, at the hotel, with special sensitivity and tea and pastry, by sympathetic hotel staff with whom we felt an immediate and unspoken connection.

Just beyond the large bay windows of the lounge in which we sat lay a huge, double swimming pool, replete with waterfalls and poolside games. It was a very hot June Tuesday. The youngsters in our group gazed at the pool with a mixture of interest and trepidation. I called them together, sensing that I had their parents' blessing. I spoke to them: "I want you to go out there and enjoy the pool. Nothing is going to happen to you. We will look out for each other. We will take turns watching each other. I know you are all heartbroken because of what happened. You must grieve, you must remember, but you must not punish yourselves. Go and enjoy the water."

The pilgrimage group that had already celebrated so much together now was faced with learning how to grieve together as well. The blunt intrusion of mortality lent us a rare opportunity that we never would have wanted but that no one in that assemblage chose to squander. Slowly, gently, with many moments of prayer and respect and clinging and group care, we concluded the pilgrimage. No one who was there, children and adults, will ever be the same again. We all look to each other, including the Londons, as kindred spirits for the rest of our days on the earth—each of which we count as a blessing.

In the months following, I heard people tell me, including many who had not been in Israel, that they looked upon their lives differently. The little boy who slipped away in the desert seemed to teach many things. "I used to get worked up over such nonsense," said one dad whom I know had been prone to bursts of impatience. "Now, when I'm about to get angry, I ask myself, what is the difference? There are always more important things."

Another family who had been in Israel with us and who had undertaken the voyage in an attempt to overcome some longstanding emotional problems, seemed to gain much more insight than they might have otherwise. In spite of serious difficulty, and a lack of trust that had brewed among the parents and children of this family, the mother reported to me later in the summer that "we seem to really understand each other again." "I'm not taking anything for granted anymore," said the father. "Not my kids. Not anything."

Others in the community, some of whom did not know Michael and his family, discovered a new awareness. "I was about to yell at my kid because she had gained some weight," a mother admitted to me later that summer. "All of a sudden I realized how stupid that was. I've stopped caring about her clothes and all that. I think about just having her to hold in the first place. What was I so obsessed about all these years?"

Michael London, a little boy, was not able to arrange peace with his mortality, although most of us who knew about him made adjustments in life as a result of that knowledge. Meanwhile, Lanie Barnes, a woman in trouble, was making an exceptional agreement with her mortality and that of her child, even as the London family had made plans to embark on their fateful journey.

Lanie's friend Vern says that Lanie was "a woman full of life with a will to live stronger than any that I've known." Vern shared the story, clearly moved and affected by the fortitude of another, relatively young adult who possessed a lot more audacity than most people can even hypothesize.

As people do, Lanie made a mistake in marriage. She met and married a man in Chicago who fooled her. Lanie's husband tended to drink heavily, and he found relief for his afflictions in acts of cruelty directed against his wife. The marriage was filled with abuse and sorrow, yet somehow produced a treasured first child named James.

Now Lanie made the second of her fateful choices. Vern reported: "Faced with perhaps the most difficult decision she ever *thought* she'd have to face, that of raising her son without a father or raising him with less than a loving father, she tried everything that she knew to repair her marriage."

Lanie's mother was a psychiatrist whose second marriage was to another psychiatrist. "She thought she had immediate access to the whole bag of tricks," said Vern, "but it wasn't meant to be." The two psychiatrists divorced after a relatively short marriage, and Lanie was again left to her own devices. "She kept on trying to collect the pieces and put Humpty Dumpty—her marriage—back together again," said Vern with sadness. Meanwhile, James remained the light of her increasingly complicated existence, as Lanie began to negotiate issues that would try any good person's spirit.

After a strenuous few more months, Lanie discovered that she was, in fact, carrying another child. "I can't imagine that it was a planned pregnancy," Vern speculated. "I do know, however, the pressure was on to make things work." But Lanie eventually resigned herself to raising two children basically without a father. In her ruminations, she could not have imagined the questions that still lay ahead.

In my work as a rabbi, I am sometimes asked why certain people are confronted with so many adversities and tragedies, while others live quiet, long lives. There is something to the old lament that life breaks unevenly for people; that it is unfair. I suppose that matters are made even in some sphere beyond our perception. After Patty and Alan London suffered the incomprehensible death of their son Michael, I advised their other children, and all the many children who sat in shock at Michael's funeral: "Ultimately, a circumstance, not God, took Michael; God, not a circumstance, will teach us to live without him."

Nevertheless, the circumstances of Lanie Barnes took on new, ominous layers. A diagnosis of breast cancer came within a few months of the pregnancy. She was advised to have the affected tissue surgically removed and then follow a protocol of chemotherapy. Lanie, so very much alone in her determinations, resolved that a mastectomy could solve the whole problem and would not threaten her unborn child. She looked into her son Jamie's eyes, and made her judgment. She had her breast removed.

Vern tenderly recalled Lanie's dilemma: "She felt very self-conscious after the operation. She wore baggy clothes, worked out at the gym, kept her spirits up. She ate all sorts of beans, leaves, herbs, super shakes, and things that I still have no idea what they were."

But Lanie still had to decide about the chemotherapy, because the cancer did not appear to be eradicated. If she submitted to the treatments, she would likely be unable to carry the baby to term. If she did not, the child would have a good chance, but her own chances would be terribly diminished. Vern summarized the situation: "The question was whether to sacrifice your unborn child's life in hopes of saving your own or possibly sacrifice your own in hopes of saving your unborn child."

Vern compared this predicament to the biblical story of Abraham contemplating the sacrifice of his son, Isaac. *But Abraham didn't have cancer,* I thought to myself. Ironically, Alan London raised the same biblical parable with me the morning after Michael died in the same desert as the scriptural incident. About to part from each other at the forlorn kibbutz, Alan asked me why he had to give up his son, while Abraham was spared his son. I could only counter that Isaac, unlike Michael, was an only child, and that Alan had two children still to love and comfort. Meanwhile, thinking about Vern's story, I concluded to myself that Lanie Barnes may have had more to offer spiritually than Abraham because at least she argued with fate when faced with the sacrifice of her child.

So Lanie, minus a breast, plus her dignity, eventually gave birth to a healthy baby boy. She hoped that the tumor would recede and that she might even resume a happier life. Her husband had ignominiously departed the scene altogether; she turned for emotional sustenance to her mother, a sister who rose to the occasion, and a new boyfriend who was kind and supportive.

But, ultimately, we are solitary in our mortality, and we, alone, make fateful decisions that implicate our lives on the earth. A series of ultrasounds betrayed the relentless disease. "The cancer was back with a vengeance," said Vern. Lanie battled the illness and gathered her children to her as an ugly custody battle began over the two boys. "Still fighting," remembered Vern, "like no one I've ever known, she hung in there, strengthened with every cry, scream, and smile that adorned the faces of her children."

In the matter of mortality, how many among us pursue life while life is still flourishing, then relinquish it much more informed? How many of us, still buoyant, flush with material success, embrace our kids as Lanie did while she still had strength in her arms? It's fickle, this existence, and we so often fail to discern the meaning of parenthood, the liturgy of marriage, the poetry of our daily friendships. Lanie Barnes had a father who had gone to live in Switzerland twenty years before his daughter's final crisis, and who did not get to know his brave offspring until the closing weeks of her life. But he did so, to his credit, and to her great and closing comfort.

She died, this noble mother and teacher of human life, and a court of law mandated her two children to their father. Yet, those boys, Lanie's parents, her sister, her friends, her caregivers—all have been profoundly changed by the nature of her relationship to mortality. Even her former husband, chastened, blessed for now with their shared progeny, must have some inkling of how the woman he once loved had more answers than he had ever questions.

Vern shook his head in dismay and awe at the story shared. "Actually, what the hell do I know?" he asked.

So much that you can't imagine, sighed an angel in heaven.

It was the loneliness of death that we wanted my father-in-law to avoid. Marty Rosen, seventy-seven, easygoing, sentimental about little things, became the third of the three exemplary deaths of that long summer. Cathy, so close to her dad, dreading his imminent disappearance, had already learned much from helping to bury little Michael London. "How can I truly complain when this beautiful boy was eleven, and my father is as old as he is?" I knew she meant it intellectually, but I also knew she suffered emotionally beyond measure.

The cancer began in his esophagus—a certain irony, given his fondness for distinctive cuisine, and his cultivated pursuit of a good Rhine wine. Marty had always swallowed life so easily; now the strapping golfer with an ivory smile and strong chin would be able to swallow almost nothing. His weight loss, exacerbated by intrusive treatments, was expedited mercilessly by the fact that his throat, his stomach, his very being were being eaten rather than him eating. Others had surely died around Marty—during his childhood; during the Second World War, in which he served in Italy; in the booming postwar years of his initial entrepreneurial success; in the later, waning years he spent surrounded by his tender gang of family, friends, and associates. He'd surrendered his parents, as we all do, and he eventually lost his brother and his sister, whom he simply adored.

But Marty just didn't seem like *he* was ever supposed to die; he just kept on wearing those cashmere V-neck sweaters and those gabardine slacks, keeping tabs on Jack Nicklaus, evaluating the retail culture, digesting *USA Today*, humming Vicki Carr songs, listening to Frank Sinatra, and recalling—for the rest of us—what we imagined was that vanished, Rat Pack ambiance of brisk sentimentality, bubbly camaraderie, and brash American optimism.

Only a few months before the sudden onset of his ailment, Marty, who had never really been ill before, announced, without boastfulness, "I will probably live for another fifteen or twenty years." None of us doubted it; Marty didn't ask too much of heaven, and there appeared to be no reason for God to be angry with or even focused upon this nice man.

It wasn't as though my father-in-law had never lost anything, or not suffered adversity. Indeed, he had known bouts of loss—in business, in social status, in more than a few gambling adventures. But none of it seemed to cost him his spirit. The fact is that his most dramatic setback was the product of his own calculation and will: Marty Rosen deliberately squandered a significant part of his business capital, when, in 1968, he made the decision to relinquish all the guns that were being sold at his discount department stores in his native Columbus, Ohio.

In general, it was the spiraling urban violence of the United States that pricked Marty's conscience: He couldn't help but wonder if one or more people—maybe even kids—had been killed by guns or bullets purchased from his stock. Specifically, it was the murder of Robert F. Kennedy, just weeks after that of Dr. Martin Luther King, Jr., that affected and roused Marty. Not far beneath his pleasant demeanor was, as it turned out, a brooding anger about social injustice and uncivilized behavior. Marty called the city police department and requested that his firearms be collected.

The action prompted much admiration, as well as significant cynicism, some disgust from other businesspeople, hate mail from social bigots, and a memorable burst of national publicity. National newsmagazines reported on Marty's action and he appeared for a lengthy

interview on NBC's *Huntley-Brinkley Report*. None of the attention particularly affected Marty; he just did what he thought he should do,
and pretty much accepted the various consequences. One could
have foretold at that point that Marty Rosen would also accept his
mortality fairly evenly when it reached for his throat a generation
after he walked away from his inventory of handguns and rifles.

"I'm not angry about all of this," he told Cathy and me just weeks
before his death. Marty perceived the changing of the seasons. Just
four months before his initial diagnosis, he had calmly and unceremoniously written a compact retirement memo to all of his employees
and co-workers at the commercial uniform company that he then
managed. The note began, simply: "My internal clock tells me it is
time to make a change."

Now, near the end, he sat in his accustomed lounge chair, surrounded by his usual magazines, newspapers, and three interacting
television/VCR remote controls. He was dreadfully thin, intermittently coherent, and, because of the morphine and the apprehension,
sometimes uncharacteristically harsh in his assessments of the people
around him. Short on flesh, out of options, he would occasionally
inveigh against my mother-in-law for her "interference," and against
his three daughters for "sticking your noses in my business." It was as
understandable as it was heartbreaking. In sweeter, more lucid moments,
he wished he could have been granted more time to see his grandchildren. But he wasn't going to bargain with heaven. And we knew,
while working with the angelic hospice nurses who came to the
house, and praying for his gentle release from this terminal labyrinth,
that heaven wasn't going to make a deal even with this seemly man
who proved mortal after all.

"Let me be who I am" was the declared motif of one of the hospice
newsletters we read during the closing days of my father-in-law's life.
The beneficent servants of the agency came to the house with their
quiet advice, their special ability to listen, their compassion for
Marty, their philosophy, their medications, their breathing exercises,
their prayers. They helped to change beds, assisted my beleaguered
and worried mother-in-law with errands and deliveries, discreetly
answered our anxious inquiries about "what's next?" or "how long?"

They helped calm Marty with assurance and direction; they taught us to make him feel that he remained in control of his life. They were there with meals, fluids, lists, drugs, statements of patient rights, living wills.

When my mother-in-law, nervously charged to administer certain drugs, asked what to do if Marty appeared to succumb during the middle of the night, the hospice nurse advised her *not* to dial 911. "They will come here and revive him," she alerted us. That was not Marty's wish, nor ours, any longer. Soon, Marty was not ours anymore either.

In the days after his death, I found a handwritten note to my father-in-law from Robin, the hospice nurse. It touched me deeply: "Enclosed is the information about the hospice which you requested," the note began. "I hope you find it helpful. . . . Wishing you all the best as you make these tough decisions."

Why did Marty Rosen make peace with his mortality so soon after announcing that he was going to keep on living? *He* had contacted the hospice people himself. *He* was going to make the tough decisions—or at least believe that he was. He had taken the initiative on the handguns. He had been blessed with fifty-four years of marriage. He organized his thoughts, arranged his business, took his risks, said his prayers. Somehow, when the end came—as much at his direction as anybody else's—he was allowed to continue being himself.

In the course of a few months on this earth, in between the spring and autumn solstices, three people came to mortality. A little boy lost his life, a mother traded her life, a grandfather finished his life. It happens all around us, and it will happen to each one of us. The difference lies in what we make of the value of life.

Meanwhile, it was during the fall that preceded that spring and summer when Emma Bennett took her seat in the sanctuary of her synagogue. She had a strong feeling that these would be her last High Holy Days on earth. She had been through the gamut of treatments, nausea, recoveries, wigs. Yet she felt sure of herself. Her husband, Jimmy, who loved her fiercely and who took every breath with her, joined her in the pews, handing her a prayerbook. She told me about her thoughts that day.

Adenocarcinoma of the peritoneum, she thought to herself. It was a cancer that had to do with her lungs. *That's what I have. But that's not who I am.* She took Jimmy's hand, shut her eyes, and listened to the organ prelude that filled the old tabernacle. She had written in her journal, just before the holiday: "As cancer patients, the only control we have is knowledge."

She thought about her lifelong quest for knowledge. She remembered the day decades before, upon graduating high school at age sixteen, when she decided to leave tiny Thorold, in Ontario, and make her way to East Liverpool, Ohio. She had been accepted to a nursing school there. Now Emma smiled to herself. The reason for her departure had ostensibly been because there was no such nursing program for someone her age in Ontario. But there was more to it, and it had to do with two fellows who pursued her—both of whom were strongly disapproved of by Emma's mother. Life had been interesting, thought Emma to herself with a sigh and another squeeze of Jimmy's warm hand. "Challenges are like chocolates," she had also declared in her journal. "Once I get a taste, I never seem to get enough."

Now she opened her prayerbook, turning to a random section in the morning service. Her hands trembled a bit, and her eyes grew misty, as she read the following on the page before her:

> On Rosh Hashanah it is written,
> on Yom Kippur it is sealed:
> How many shall pass on, how many shall come to be;
> who shall live and who shall die;
> who shall see ripe age and who shall not;
> who shall perish by fire and who by water;
> who by sword and who by beast;
> who by hunger and who by thirst;
> who by earthquake and who by plague;
> who by strangling and who by stoning;
> who shall be secure and who shall be driven;

who shall be tranquil and who shall be troubled;
who shall be poor and who shall be rich;
who shall be humbled and who exalted.

Maybe, thought Emma. *Maybe—as long as my handwriting is in that book.*

Chapter Four

Visiting in the Culture of Death

QUIET PLEASE
Service in Progress

The sign, though momentarily off to the side, is nonetheless visible as I enter the foyer of the Berkowitz-Kumin-Bookatz Memorial Chapel in Cleveland Heights, Ohio. My eye, however, is drawn to the ceiling-directed tree, set in a large vase under a skylight, which extends upward from a circular couch in the middle of the primarily gray and white room. Hope, light, and the circle of life are communicated to me, although I am keenly aware that this is a funeral home.

Indeed, the whole pale picture, intended to send one's hopes aloft, is nonetheless pulled in an ominous direction by the long, downward-thrusting staircase that drags the locus of the room away from the tree and the heaven and toward, well, something below. I understand that the suspect stairway goes down to administrative offices but can't shake the feeling that the stairs lead down to something more forbidding.

Barnett Bookatz, in his mid-forties, solidly built, bearded, with sympathetic eyes, appears in the room. His suit and tie blend impeccably against his compact chest; the room with the tree seems more animated with his arrival. Bart, as he is called, has been a licensed funeral director since 1972, and this busy building, the preeminent

Jewish funeral home in the community, is his workplace. Decorously, Bart extends his warm hand, then offers me an official Jewish calendar, replete with weekly Torah portion citations and the Sabbath candle lighting schedules. Bart's world turns on time, and he is a magistrate of the world clock.

Settling into his somewhat cramped office at the base of those ultimately innocent stairs, I ask Bart about his work.

His response is immediate: "It is all-consuming, and has a great emotional and physical impact on me." We sit facing each other, opposite his desk, which, like the wall, is laden with manifold community awards and honors. Bart, keeper of the dead, is committed to the welfare of the living. Beneath his framed official license as a funeral director are medallions and plaques and citations from synagogue brotherhoods, Israel Bonds, the regional Bereavement Council, the Hebrew Free Loan Society, Big Brothers, Shoes for Kids, the Rape Crisis Center, the Russian Resettlement Committee, Alzheimer's Association, a local chaplaincy, and a variety of others.

Bart proceeds to explain the burden that transfers to him after any single death. "To arrange a funeral generally involves ten to twelve hours," he says. Bart notes the extensive coordination required among family members, clergy, and the cemetery administration. All this happens in an environment of fresh grief. "But first, they call the funeral director. There is a trained person here in this building twenty-four hours a day. We don't have or believe in an answering service. Deaths occur at any time. I am phoned at all hours of the day or night. Our job is to immediately give survivors reassurance, and then to organize the next few days of their lives." The non-Jewish funeral directors have less pressure on them, Bart submits with a smile, because Jewish funerals generally take place within a day or so of the actual death. "They have three or four days to prepare it all," Bart clarifies about his Gentile colleagues.

Bart is responsible for retrieving and transporting the body from wherever it is, writing and releasing obituary notices to the press, establishing which religious rites are applicable, and arranging the death certificate. Will there be a viewing of the body prior to the service? Will the grave be ready? Is there going to be a protective vault involved in addition to the casket?

"Funerals are for the living," Bart emphasizes. The living, acknowledging their dead, come to see him in this same office. "The members of the family," he tells me, "are confronting a lot of things. Some of them don't have as much experience with this as others do. I have to explain and propose religious rituals to them, and they don't always agree with each other." Bart recounts that a woman had just been in earlier, along with her adult son. Their husband and father had just died from Parkinson's disease. "The woman was quite negative on religion. But the son, like many children at such a time, needed religion. I worked out a series of compromises that I hope will satisfy both of them in their grief."

Bart often gestures toward the empty couch that sits between us as we speak. Numerous dramas occur on and around that piece of furniture. A kind of resting place for despairing persons, it was wrinkled with emotions, stained by tears, bent by anger, pressed by secrets. "I've seen and heard many things in here," says the seasoned funeral director, his eyes blinking with acquired wisdom. A purveyor of pathology, microbiology, social security law, accounting principles, veteran benefits, and biohazard wastes, Bart Bookatz is ultimately a manager of mortality, a human coda in a world growing increasingly unaccustomed to limits.

Before continuing our discussion in his office, Bart takes me on a tour of the facility. He glows with purpose as we enter the Death Education Library—a softly lit room just adjacent to the casket showcase chamber. The library is filled with books, pamphlets, and videos about mourning, bereavement, healing, and sharing. The director, himself the father of two teenage boys, has a delicate spot in his heart for the needs of children. In our conversation, he has already expressed his particular and keen and clinging anguish about dealing with children who have died. Today, Bart is instructive, obliging, proud, somewhat clinical; in other situations when we were working together, I've seen him turn away for a moment, rubbing his beard in agony, drying his eyes.

"Many of the hospice people use this library. And family members who are doing the right thing—pre-planning for a funeral." Bart then hands me an unused coloring book for kids entitled *Kolie and the Funeral*. There are "helpful hints" for grown-ups on the inside back cover; Bart often gives the book and some crayons to children experiencing the death of a loved one. It abounds with happy and sad drawings of "a little koala named Kolie . . . One day Kolie's Mama told him that his Grandpa had died." There were subsequent sketches, to be filled in by a child's colors and emotions, of a sad koala family, a funeral home, a casket, the deceased grandfather koala at rest in his open coffin, a hearse entering the Koalaville Cemetery, the little koala visiting the grave after the funeral. Bart passed this coloring book to me as though he were transferring scripture.

We enter the next room, which is filled with coffins on display. "This is where reality hits," Bart tells me. The fancy boxes, furnished with linings and pillows, sit open, gaping with vacancy. In this room, raw terror has flared, denial has been blunted, and, ultimately, deals have been closed. Bart points to a certain, particularly expensive casket, and says: "President Kennedy was buried in this exact model." The price is equivalent to that of a luxury automobile.

Though no stranger to these items, I examined and touched the various models, including Tigereye Bronze, Fawn Stainless Steel, Grecian Copper, Star Quartz, Neapolitan Blue, Revere Silver, Emeraldtone, and an entire category of "solid hardwoods" (mahogany, birch, poplar, oak). The caskets were laced with a choice of velvets, crepes, and a selection of stains. The least expensive were cloth-covered or pine boxes. The overall price range for the caskets was from less than one hundred dollars to many thousands of dollars. Several of the models were named for the biblical tribes and a written disclaimer found in the showroom indicated that "neither this funeral establishment nor any of its employees represents or implies that any casket will be air tight or water tight or will provide long-term preservation of human remains."

Also on display for discussion and sale were examples of outer burial containers or vaults "so the grave does not sink in." Prices were higher for Sunday or holiday installation. I thought that the entire presentation of an absolutely necessary and fundamental consumer operation was dignified and restrained. I didn't really know of any other way for a person like Bart to demonstrate his goods and services. "It's in this room, with the casket nearby, that I discuss with the family what clothes their loved one will wear," he adds.

A separate, general price list itemized the costs for an astonishing array of often essential ministrations performed by the funeral agency. These included embalming, refrigeration, bathing and handling, dressing and casketing, transferring of the body to or from airport or mortuary (night transportation was higher), floral arranging, cremating, urns, the funeral vehicle, the family vehicle, the service vehicle, shrouds, blankets, memorial books, acknowledgment cards, temporary grave markers, candles, pallbearer gloves. "In all of this," Bart notes, "we have to take precautions in handling everything. We're concerned about AIDS, hepatitis, airborne viruses. This is complicated work." During the course of business, however, Bart and his fellow morticians normally operate from computer terminals set at their desks, even as they are swept up in the most basic and human of enterprises.

Donning the required disposable garments, Bart and I enter the purification room. This is the domain of the Jewish Sacred Society, known as *chevra kaddisha*, whose volunteers devote hours to the washing and preparation of corpses. A wooden, ladder-style board lies flat across a hospital-type table. This is where the deceased is reverently placed as volunteers, avoiding conversation, chant psalms while—in strict regulation—applying water, vinegar, and egg to the dead body. The body is never left alone from the time of death until the funeral; one individual is designated as the official "watchman."

The members of the devout Sacred Society actually begin their work before the body arrives at the mortuary. When present at the scene of death, the volunteers are charged to gently lower the deceased from the deathbed within twenty minutes of actual demise, undressing, cleaning, and covering the body with a pure sheet. Some straw is placed on the ground or floor to receive the corpse. The instructions are that the body is always on its back, never turned over, and handled with extreme dignity. In deference to the departing soul, the feet always face the door of the room, and the windows are opened. A prayer is repeated while the body is lowered: "*O house of Jacob, come and let us go in the light of the lord. God has spoken and called the earth from the rising of the sun and into its setting. He enters into peace, they rest on their beds, each one that walks in his uprightness. For dust you are, and unto dust shall you return.*"

The members of the society close the eyelids of the deceased, and straighten all the limbs. A pillow is placed under the head. Candles are lit, and the body remains shrouded at all times. No one other than society members may view the body, except in cases of necessary identification.

On occasion, I have spoken with members of this Sacred Society, who perform their duties within the more observant Jewish community, about what they do. They are generally dutiful and circumspect about the whole thing. I have found them to be among the most well-adjusted people I have ever met in the matter of their own mortality. They've seen it; what is there to fear?

As we return to his office, I ask Bart if he himself handles the bodies that arrive at his building. "I certainly have, and I certainly still do," he replies. He often looks at the bodies, he explains, so that he can answer specific questions put to him by family members. What does he see when he gazes at the bodies?

"I sometimes wonder, when I look at an elderly person, shriveled, in the fetal position, what we were trying to prove by keeping this person alive. Who was really being satisfied?" I sense that Bart perhaps feels that modern civilization, obsessed with life extension, was clouding the atmosphere a bit. People who may not actually want or need to live any longer are being forced to exist nonetheless.

Bart then recalled a particular case that I knew of as well from our shared professional experience. A youthful, middle-aged woman, in life so vital, attractive, wonderfully maternal, had finally succumbed to cancer and was brought to the funeral home. Bart was shaken and affected by what he saw in the preparation room. Her face had been ravaged; she was sunken in and vanquished by the compelled extension of her doomed existence. "For what?" the funeral director now asked me. "Are the machines really doing us a favor by forcing people to keep on living lives that promise no quality?" Bart asserted that the families suffer even more in these circumstances, because they are ultimately betrayed by the *illusion* of hope.

"Then they rationalize it all even further by saying that the death was 'a blessing.' " lamented the funeral director. "What blessing? A death is a death, but the forced extension of life makes the loss that much harder later—when they realize that the person died nevertheless." Bart decries the notion of a person being "in a better place." With conviction, he expresses his concern that people routinely neglect the possibility of making *this* life "the better place." Peace, he feels, is "the end of misery, the end of sensory perception. It's not a reward you get for fighting a terrible disease or suffering a fatal accident. We should see the reward as having life in the first place. We should help each other here and now. Do the good here. Don't cop out and hope to do it in some next world. When I see the dead bodies that come here, I don't think that God created us into some kind of stepping-stone. This is life, now. People shouldn't put off making the best of it while they're alive because they or somebody else believes that the reward is later."

What has his work taught Bart about mortality?

"I don't get too excited about most things," he chuckles softly. "It sometimes drives my wife crazy, but I just don't get all that worked up about a dry-cleaning order that was mixed up, or if my landscaper didn't exactly do a great job. I may be too laid back because of what I see here, and I may have a tendency to put off decisions about future things. But I can't help it. It's usually not worth it. We can't really plan all that much. I think I appreciate life in a way others don't."

Bart pauses for a moment. He cups his hands and smiles. "I must tell you that I see a lot of bull. There is this myth of 'the perfect family.' No such thing. I mediate among family members all the time when somebody dies." His face tightens: "Especially when a child dies in a divorce situation. The parents fight over where and how the child will be buried. When people get divorced, they should just get divorced. But they keep on fighting with each other, on and on. What's the point? People waste so much time and energy."

The director is now light-years away from accounting procedures, transport permits, and forensic licenses. "I do believe in a first creator, a maker of life. Look, I was originally burying strangers. The years have passed. I began burying the parents of people I know and love, then their spouses, their friends, even their children. I'm a father myself. I value life. I try to make it mean something."

Bart's phone rings, startling both of us. He picks up the receiver and listens. "I'm so sorry," he says. "I'll be over shortly. I knew your father. He was a good man."

A process begins, an agency mobilizes. A life has ended, and several other lives, including that of Barnett Bookatz, are about to be further illuminated.

"I was a son of the nineteen-sixties, probably like you, Rabbi," says the police sergeant. Jeff Porter, forty-five years old, the father of three small children, remembers coming of age knighted with idealism and the belief that a person could change the world. After almost twenty years "in the streets," he is not so certain. He has seen life and death interplay, sometimes violently, and he worries about how the human family is handling itself.

He is burly, outgoing, and, like a police bullet, sometimes very direct. "What's my philosophy on life?" He responds to my query. "Simple: Every day above ground is a great day."

He is not normally in any kind of mortal danger, having acceded to the records bureau of his suburban police department in northeastern Ohio. Porter maintains and processes a file system on all reported crimes, investigations, and arrests that occur within his district. "I've been behind this desk for two years now, but spent my first nineteen out there. I saw a lot of things that have made me think."

"So you were involved with acts of violence or tragedy?" I ask.

"Oh, yes. I mean, this is not an inner-city department, so you can imagine that what we see here doesn't compare to what a city police officer is up against daily." *I really can only imagine,* I think to myself, but find this policeman philosophic enough to indicate that he has passed through plenty of revealing encounters. He proceeds to offer a litany of D.O.A.s, suicides, and traffic fatalities to which he has responded over the years. "I cannot believe what people sometimes do to each other or to themselves," he remarks. I sense that he has really put in his time and service in the culture of embroilment, and is quite grateful now for the desk job.

What did the street teach him?

"Live life to the fullest, for the love of God," he tells me. He is truly pensive, a thinker with a badge. "Look," he continues, almost feverishly. "I don't like what's happened to me in some ways. I don't like people anymore. Can you imagine? I mean, I came out of that period of idealism, the sixties, really sure that a person could make a difference. I dreamed of serving as a policeman. Well, I did, but it's changed me so much. The things I've seen have made me care a lot more about my family, my life, and I still think of myself as a 'people person.' But I don't like people. Nobody can please me."

I know that Sergeant Porter is being hard on himself, because he is clearly a generous and agreeable man. But it is also clear that he carries a certain pain, a disconsolation about things that registers through his outwardly sunny disposition. I am certainly not one to judge; the sergeant may be dispatching officers and messages and material now, but his hands have obviously been washed clean from blood and despair that soiled him for far too long and in too many street corners, alleyways, storefronts, and living rooms.

"Our society," he states plainly, "has gone bad." He shakes his head, sighing, looking for some elusive contentment. "We are pretty bad for our fellow man," he declares, sounding a bit like a tin prophet in uniform. But I really like him, and feel that he has a legitimate right to preach, founded upon some serious and haunting memories.

Porter blames the media for much of the malaise that leads people to consider guns, drugs, cruelty, and extortion in their surge for control. He laments the coarse disclosure of such particulars to young people across the television and cinematic screens of our country. I sense that he originally became a police officer because he genuinely wanted to help mitigate civilization and to protect people in their mortality; his experience with the human spirit obviously betrayed the proclivity of too many humans for recklessness.

Yet it certainly has taught him something. I ask him what his worst memory is, expecting to hear some horror story about a shooting or a heinous hit-and-run car accident. In fact, his worst memory is horrifying, but it does not emanate from the streets, nor from the report of a handgun. It is the loss of a fellow police officer three weeks prior from natural causes. Sergeant Porter's colleague suffered a fatal heart attack, and Porter got the call.

"I had to go over to the house and wake up his family at three o'clock in the morning. It was so awful. I worked through for twelve hours, helping to make all the arrangements, trying to comfort his family. It was a real loss for all of us."

The policeman emphasizes the word *real*. Surely, the loss of a comrade is authentic and urgent. But, without a doubt, Sergeant Porter's nineteen years of exposure to the raw edges of mortality made this loss all the more real, and his dutiful and sensitive response all the more so part of his *worst* memory.

In Deer Park, a suburb of Houston, Detective Dana Belmont has memories as well. I first met Dana in the early eighties, when she managed a huge, corporate hotel in downtown Houston. Reddish in complexion, with wavy, chestnut hair, Dana was at the time engaged to the security officer of the hotel. She was young then, full of élan vital, considerably enamored of her boyfriend's work as well as his person. My interaction with her was brief and professional; I was organizing a conference of rabbis in Houston and she was my contact. We discovered that we both had grown up in Cincinnati, adding to the very amicable discourse that brightened our business together. Dana Belmont told me that she was enrolled in some criminology courses at Texas Southern University and that she wanted to become a police officer. "I can make a difference," I remember her saying to me back then. "Maybe I can save some lives."

Now, fourteen years later, Dana's voice at the other end of the line sounded somewhat weary. She was a robbery and homicide detective, with some rank and a considerable amount of experience. Her onetime fiancé had long ago departed the scene. "He ran away the minute I got a gun and a badge. It seems that he didn't want to share this kind of life with me. Or maybe he just couldn't handle the fact that I was also in this line of work." She sounded, if not bitter, resigned—to a number of things.

"Why did you stay down there?" I asked.

"Well, don't you know?" She laughed sarcastically. "It's the bluebonnets and the mockingbirds we've got down here." I recalled her lively sense of humor, although it sounded somewhat deflated. She told me then that she really couldn't quit the scene due to a fairly good pension plan, and that she was doing what she had wanted to do. Moreover, Dana was something of the computer expert in her bureau, and was working on a new software system that could help trace offenders. "We're not a real big department, and I sort of get involved with a number of facets around here," she announced in her euphonious southern inflection.

Resourceful, smart, still energetic, Dana mentioned that she is also a specialist in fingerprint technology. "We just got this new machine. It's called a True-Touch and it does wonders. The system is cutting-edge, and involves none of the old, inky mess. We can really connect people to situations like we never have before."

"Dana, have you ever killed anybody?" I wanted to know.

"Yes. One person." The explicatory monotone in her voice vanished. The line was momentarily quiet. I pictured her as I remembered her fourteen years earlier, cheerfully signing documents and offering me the courtesy of an upgrade in my accommodations at her hotel. That memory was so benign; her current reality was so malignant.

It was a necessary and "clean hit," Dana explained to me unapologetically. There had been a break-in and robbery attempt at a private residence. "It happened around Christmastime last year, in a fancy neighborhood," she said, explaining that some bad or indigent people get reckless and some good people get careless during what police recognize as an intense, often dangerous season.

Dana and her male partner were called in response to a security alarm just after dawn. They were told that the two intruders were quite possibly armed. "We just had the light on the dashboard of the car, no siren. But two other marked patrol cars also approached, their sirens going. The two guys came running out of a side door as we pulled into the driveway. One ran off to the back of the house. One of our guys nabbed him on foot within minutes. But the other guy, the other bad guy—he saw me and my partner and fired a shot. I do remember actually feeling it whisk past my ear and then it hit the roof of our car. It ricocheted off the car and slammed into a tree. For some strange reason, I remember thinking about the dry branches of this tree crumpling down, and thinking about what a waste that was, when I aimed and pulled the trigger. I don't recall pulling my gun out or much of anything else. I just remember—you know, I love to garden, and I love the cypress trees down here—I just remember being upset about that tree. Then, the guy was down on the drive-way and I just was staring at him from where I stood. Then I kept thinking, God, now I am a killer, too. My partner ran past me, practically knocking me down, and pointed his gun right into the guy's head. He was just checking to make sure everything was okay, but I kept thinking, don't kill him again, he can only die once. I didn't get too close to the scene. I was surprised there wasn't much blood at all. The whole family was home when these two idiots decided to break in. A mom and a dad and three kids. They wouldn't come out until a bunch of other officers came over and went in to see them, including a psychologist. They didn't want to talk to me and I didn't want to talk to them. The guy shot at me! So I did what I was supposed to do. There was a formal inquiry, and frankly, everybody was great about it. I'm considered some kind of hero by some, not all. It's something I'll never forget, and it does bother me at night sometimes. I've had some bad dreams. I've talked to someone about it. I think what bothers me is that I feel that we're all like that poor cypress tree innocently growing out of the earth, and all of a sudden a terrible, hot, destructive thing comes barreling in, bouncing off a car, no less!"

"Do you feel guilt about this, Dana?" I asked.

"Of course I do. My mother, an old-time Nazarene, taught me to respect life. I love the earth and the blossoms, the smell of pine. I think sometimes: What am I doing mixing in with this business? It's God's work, who lives and who dies. And then I come along and, in the line of duty, take a life."

"He was going to take yours," I offered, certain this was a cliché.

"Look, I know that. A lot of people can take my life. I'm afraid to go out too much with people. My hands get into blood and fluids and God knows what. I've tested myself for HIV so many times I can't keep track. The men I work with are mostly divorced, miserable, unsure of themselves, suspicious about everything. The relationships I've had have all been short. Some guys are just interested in my gun, or in the fact that I killed that person. People get crazy when they have too much power over other people's lives. It's too bad we have to have it this way. God, how I wish life could be like it is for the big pines. They come out of the earth, grow under the sky, take in the sunlight, and they rot quietly and naturally. We don't have that kind of peace. We just run over each other. The other day, I was issued a new kind of control baton to take with me when I'm walking through a tough area. I can now knock somebody down who is stronger than me, and this kind of stick is versatile and flexible enough, they tell me, so that it won't break bones. That, you see, can minimize lawsuits from the people we have to restrain. I don't have too much faith in human nature, and my biggest disappointment is how we just don't care about life."

Steven Fink, a rabbi and police chaplain in Des Moines, Iowa, told me: "What I find to be most profound is the distress, usually in the form of post-traumatic shock, that comes to an officer after he or she fires a weapon and kills a perpetrator. There is real grief in this. They feel very vulnerable to death on duty and as those who can dispense death. They are emotional and sensitive about these things."

I spoke to Dana Belmont once again, about a month later. She revealed to me during this second conversation that she has an eleven-year-old daughter who is in day care most of the time. "My old boyfriend from the hotel left me something good," she said. She had decided to leave the police department and go into private security work, "mostly on computers." She had determined that her professional exposure to life and death was simply too much of a risk for her daughter's well-being. "Life is too fragile," she told me. "I realize that I'm not breathing it in through my nostrils. It's crawling under my skin. Life is too fragile to be experienced like that. I'd also like, while I'm still alive, to get some real love."

I hung up the phone, realizing that I had been talking to a composed, focused, if unhappy woman who—even with the unspeakable burden of having legally taken a human life—understands human life in more ways than most.

The brittleness of life is what Reverend Joseph Hilinski thinks about almost every day. Hilinski, the director of interfaith activities for the Cleveland Catholic Diocese, is also a parish priest. "I'm amazed by the twists and turns of life, and I don't mean this in the emotional sense," said the clergyman.

"Just last week," he continued, "a parishioner of mine went into the emergency room for what appeared to be something routine. Forty-five minutes later he was dead. This made a deep impression on me. I wish people would stop expecting each other to be so strong, and stop being so surprised when one of us does reveal our frailties. We're not made of stainless steel. If we looked at each other for what we are—fragile and vulnerable and certainly mortal—we wouldn't get so disappointed in one another for not being infallible. I sometimes think it would be good if people could permanently wear the same kind of outer tag that a lot of appliance packages have: FRAGILE—HANDLE WITH CARE."

Brenda, an emergency room nurse at a large medical facility in the Midwest, would likely agree. "I see it all, in ten- or twelve-hour shifts," she told me. "People just don't understand that they are breakable, and very susceptible." Brenda, patching and suturing and repairing and losing mortal beings, inhabits an environment that swirls swiftly and technically—across heart monitors and blood pressure gauges and oxygen machines—in and out of the lines of mortality. I spoke to her just after she changed the tubing for someone's intravenous connection; the IV had been improperly connected. The patient complained of chest pains and a headache. Brenda administered acetaminophen tablets for the headache. "It's caused by the nitro patch you're wearing, honey," she explained to the patient. Brenda, thirtyish, olive-skinned, extremely kind, accommodating, wore all whites, carried some basic medical instruments, and brandished bright silver nail polish. Her world was sterilized, but it was not going to be sterile.

Her humanity came through, even as she swept through a maze of suction canisters, nebulizers, twill tape, vessel trays, neck rolls, line kits, blood tubes, dressings, gloves, and restraints. We spoke against a human din that came from the next cubicle: Bonita, a demolished human remnant, shrieked and cursed incessantly and incoherently as she lay crashing from an overdose of crack cocaine.

Brenda rolled her eyes in acknowledgment of the sound, but went on about her business. Human life, wounded, invaded, fractured, attacked, poisoned, lay about in equal quarters across the cots and tables of this emergency sector. Brenda said: "This is my life. Things happen to people all day and all night. A lot of folks get religion more from here than from being in church. This is where you find out how defenseless you really are. I just always hope that first, people go on from here to a regular hospital bed or back home and recover, and that second, they learn something about themselves from it all."

The nurse and I spoke briefly about Chris Farley, the actor and comedian who had just been found dead that same day in his Chicago apartment. Farley, thirty-three years old, an alumnus of *Saturday Night Live* and an emerging movie star, rotund, extravagant, and truly funny, evidently died from personal indulgence and a lack of discipline. "He made me laugh," said Brenda. "What a shame. He didn't even get to an emergency room."

The *New York Times* reported on the death of Chris Farley the next morning, offering a revealing comment from the brilliant but doomed young comic. In a magazine article published just three months before his death, Farley had stated: "I used to think that you could get to a level of success where the laws of the universe didn't apply. . . . Once I thought that if I had enough in the bank, if I had enough fame, then it would be all right. But I'm a human being like everyone else. I'm not exempt."

Not one of us is exempt, Brenda would surely say, as she tries to comfort a screaming addict, sets the broken bone of an exuberant athlete, connects a middle-aged executive to an electrocardiogram unit, injects potassium into an older woman, wraps a body sheet around a dead teenager.

Meanwhile, a career in radiology has taught Helen Wahba a great deal about serenity. Helen, a wife and mother in her forties hailing from Louisville, Kentucky, spends a good deal of her time working in a hospital nursing unit. "I sedate people," she explained. With calm, blue eyes and a soothing disposition, Helen prepares people for MRIs and "a lot of different interventional procedures, arteriograms, biopsies, and any kind of invasive procedure where they put tubes in your kidneys, or wherever else. I see a lot of very sick people."

I asked Helen what all this exposure to mortal situations has taught her.

"It makes me look at life in a different way," she answered without hesitation. "The fact that I have spent so much time with people who were fighting death, and other people who were craving death, has made me feel more at ease with life, and with the fact of dying." The nurse, who also spent time in emergency and intensive care units, has arrived at another conclusion about the dying themselves: "I think that there are a lot of people who, when it comes time for them to die, and they know they're ready for death, they themselves have control over their bodies to the point where they can arrive at it." Helen believes, based upon the extraordinary dramas she has helped manage, that human beings for the most part are much more at ease— and in command—of their mortality than we assume or imagine.

Helen cited several cases of healthy spouses who lost their loved ones to a terminal disease, and who then essentially decided to die within a few months. (As a rabbi, I have seen this myself; in response to loneliness or other circumstances people *do* exert some dominion in the matter of life and death.) Years ago, Helen related, a gentleman who was a local television celebrity in Louisville was brought into her unit suffering from a heart attack. "His heart was in a very fragile state," she emphasized.

"For twenty-four hours after he had his heart attack, this man literally died twenty-eight times. He had to be cardioverted twenty-eight times, he went into fibrillation, and we had to go in and shock him twenty-eight times. We all were very emotionally involved with this man, because a lot of us had grown up watching him on television. He pulled through, and two years later I saw him on an interview, doing well. People are sometimes just not ready to go. There is a question of will in all this."

I asked Helen if she felt there is a spiritual dimension to all of this, and she responded that, unquestionably, there is. "I believe that people who have never had any religion or form of faith suddenly get it when they get close to death. I've seen it happen so many times. People will get a more peaceful quality about themselves when they've passed through this. I myself am very spiritual, and every time I start a procedure, even as small an item as sticking a needle in for an IV, I always say a little prayer. Especially when I'm working on little kids." Helen, born into a strict Lutheran heritage and having chosen Judaism as an adult, has no doubts, however, as to the special source of her religiosity: "I think my faith, my feeling for God, has really deepened and become a happier one since I began working my intensive care experiences. Being so much around the living and dying has given me peace."

Helen has some advice for people, learned first from her mother: "I take it to the Lord in prayer, but then I do something different. I leave it there. I figure, God's going to take care of it, I don't worry about it anymore. What would be the point of that?" She momentarily shut her eyes. Then she spoke: "I've seen a lot of things. I'm not going to spend too much time being stressed, after what I've seen."

Not every professional who is immersed in the culture of death is necessarily moved or informed or even educated. I was disappointed by the reaction of a reporter for a prominent television station in south Florida. "Sure, I see the bodies, I see the blood, and I see the carnage. But I'm sorry, it just doesn't affect me. It's what people do to each other, and it brings out who really are the sinners. I believe that Christ ordains everything, and that what happens is supposed to happen, and we journalists happen to be the ones covering it. And people want to see it, probably because it fascinates them."

"What about your own death?" I felt compelled to investigate this investigator, who seemed to turn faith into rationalization.

"That's simply going to be my reward for doing my job here on earth."

I couldn't help but feel that this woman was lucky to be telegenic, talented, and ambitious. But I certainly was concerned for her—if and when she personally runs into one of Father Hilinski's "twists and turns."

Farther north, another anchorperson has clearly grown from his exposure to mortal matters. "For years, I was untouched by other people's pain and death," confessed Ted Henry. Henry is seen daily on the ABC affiliate in Cleveland. He has an impressive array of community and social service credits, and he told me that he worries about the living, and wonders about the dead.

But Ted, by his own account, was once caught up in the sanitization of mortality brought on by the endless bombardment that we all endure, in his words: "Hollywood death, TV news death, newspaper death, radio death, best-seller death, criminal death, and so on." He was numb to it all, "no matter what the murder, no matter how grotesque or strange the circumstances."

It took the frightful story of a thirteen-year-old Hispanic girl to open Ted's heart, and to make him consider the effect of his work upon his own feelings of mortality. The girl was visiting a friend who lived next door. He, also thirteen, found a handgun in his mother's bedroom dresser and pulled it out to show the girl. Ted told me the story as though it had happened to him personally.

"The boy pulled the trigger, never expecting to find a bullet in the gun. There was one. The gun fired and the bullet struck the girl in the head. She screamed and ran out of the bedroom, down the stairs, out the front door and over to her house. Her mother heard the screams. The girl ran into her own house and up the stairs into the arms of her mother, where she died."

Ted said that when the station showed the school photograph of the "radiant" little girl, he practically fell onto his anchor desk. "My stomach muscles contracted and I could only think of my own two innocent young children." Ted Henry did not just report the wanton death of a young girl, he lived it.

The dead send us messages, from mortuaries, police stations, hospitals, hospice centers, across television monitors. When we listen, we learn. When we are exposed to death in meaningful ways, we add meaning to the concept of life. There is even lore in the cemetery.

Patrick Corrigan, a tall, athletic man with thick, long hair and a trimmed mustache, is not obsessed with his role as superintendent of the Mayfield Cemetery. The cemetery, lush and well kept, adjoins the historic Lakeview Cemetery on the heights overlooking Lake Erie, a few minutes from downtown Cleveland. Lakeview Cemetery contains the crypts of several famous people, including presidents, publishers, and the indomitable FBI agent Eliot Ness. The residents of Mayfield Cemetery, co-owned by two synagogues, include several eminent rabbis and a host of prominent German-Jewish families. Under the grass, however, the two cemeteries comprise the completely invariant story of human mortality. Bones have no pouches.

Pat, as he is called, manages the congregational cemetery, and for a time lived with his family in the house at the entrance. He supervises a crew of gravediggers, coordinates burials with the funeral agencies, maintains the landscaping, gardening, and snow-removal, and is responsible for the significant record-keeping (names, plots, dates, years) that takes place in the cemetery office. The cemetery opened in 1890; Pat has been directing there since 1977, although he began work on the grounds crew in 1969. Although still relatively young, he has a reverence for the years and for the journey of life: "All of us in our own way are pilgrims," he told me.

Pat is an accomplished photographer whose work has been showcased and exhibited. He found his way into the realm of graveyards via his camera. Watching his parents grow older, he felt the cycle of time, and found a certain placidity and reassurance while visiting and taking pictures in cemeteries. "I felt comfortable in cemeteries, I enjoyed the artwork, and found much evidence of faith."

His churchyard sojourn did not distract him from his love of motorcycling, his interest in kayaking, or his general flair for fine arts. But they did amount to a kind of spiritual quest, and he is now moved by what happens in the cemetery: "I see evidence of faith," he asserted. "I really don't have that much contact with the dead but most certainly with the living and grieving. In recent years, I have had to bury numerous persons much younger than myself. It has always been the hardest to deal with the death of the young. Facing those situations as well as watching my parents has impressed upon me the sense of urgency that each day should be lived to the fullest."

Pat Corrigan, born a Catholic, married to a Jew, is particularly impressed by a Native American doctrine that considers any day as a good day to die if one has lived properly and is ready. "This has also impressed upon me the importance of letting those close to you know how much they mean to you, how important they are in your life and you in theirs," said the man who almost daily breaks open the ground, hears prayers, stands by dutifully as people sanctify memories, and then pulls the tear-stained earth back into its place.

"Do the dead give you peace?" I inquired.

"I lived on the cemetery grounds for twelve years. I raised my children there. My wife and I together sensed, felt, and witnessed the presence of a spiritual entity from our window. And I have never been more at peace anywhere. Cemeteries are sacred grounds in the most ancient sense of the word." He is not afraid of the cemetery, he told me, because "it is the one location best suited to give us an opportunity to pause and reflect on the meaning of life and how we choose to live."

Pat Corrigan recalled a still, winter night. He opened the door of his house and took a walk in his snow-carpeted yard. The row upon row of memorial stones glistened under the light of a full moon. The great quiet soothed his soul. He told me: "My footsteps were the sole tracks in the snow yet I was never in any fear of my surroundings." Pat walked back into the warmth of his house, listening for the breathing of his loved ones. Outside, beyond his porch, the moonlight fell across a particular stone.

EMMA BENNETT
1935-1997

Chapter Five

Conversations with the Dead

At the far north end of Pat Corrigan's cemetery, beyond most of the burial plots, monuments, and at the apex of the cemetery road, stands a round, Byzantine structure known as the Mayfield Mausoleum. I have occasion to visit this building often enough; the central chapel area is frequently used for memorial services prior to burial in the cemetery itself. There are also crypts in the hallways of this catacomblike edifice for those who prefer above-ground entombment, a practice permitted in more liberal Jewish settings.

It was my duty to eulogize Dr. Joseph Tallisman one morning several years ago in the central chamber of the mausoleum. As always, the circular room was filled with souls, both seen and unseen. The living sat on folding chairs, the dead lay inside the walls. I spoke from behind the shiny casket, at a marble podium. No microphone was necessary; one's voice orbits through the spherical hall, addressing the spirits.

I adored Dr. Joseph Tallisman. "Forgive me," he would say, "but I really believe that a doctor takes care of people." Never militant, hardly assertive, he nevertheless exhibited a sense of calling about medicine. I still considered him young when he died at sixty-five years of age. His smooth face, his good nature, and his unyielding passion for the musical theatre had combined to make Joe Tallisman seemingly unassailable by the aging process.

Joe tended to burst forth with songs from as diverse a group of shows as *Gypsy*, *Cats*, and *The Sound of Music*. Visiting in his home during the final few months of his life, I didn't always need his wife, Jennifer, to direct me to him. I could find him by following the sound of his voice, coming from upstairs, declaring: *"The hills are alive. . . ."*

Joseph Tallisman had a particular fondness for Meredith Willson's *The Music Man*. I believe that he identified closely with the unrepining personality of the pivotal character, Professor Harold Hill. Dr. Tallisman could also have created a marching band out of the raw material found in his surrounding community. Joe liked to remind people that he saw the original stage production in 1958, "just after it opened, on December 19, 1957, with Robert Preston and Shirley Jones." I never had the heart to tell Joe that the female lead in 1958 was, in fact, Barbara Cook; he was confusing the Broadway show with the subsequent movie. He did know that the stage production ran for 1,375 performances and that its romantic musical number, "Goodnight, My Someone," actually had the same melody, realized at a slower rhythm, as the play's more famous and broader-cadenced "76 Trombones."

"Goodnight, my someone . . ." Joe would intone, just to demonstrate this fact. He would then immediately follow with an imaginary twirl of a drum major's baton, and a blasting of *"Seventy-six trombones led the big parade!"*

Joe also liked the beat and tune of the show's paean to the town of Gary, Indiana. He knew enough about musical measures to even correctly emphasize the number's phonic accents, carefully enunciating the phrase *"GA-ry Indi-A-na."*

Lyrics, compositions, and show tunes went through my mind as I spoke Dr. Joseph Tallisman's eulogy that day inside the Mayfield Mausoleum. He had truly been an enchanting human being, light in tone, serious in commitment, sworn to the education and cultivation of his children and grandchildren. Now, as the memorial service concluded, the general congregation was momentarily dismissed. Only Joe's immediate family accompanied me and his coffin down a hallway to the site of his crypt. There, Bart Bookatz, the funeral director, and Pat Corrigan, the cemetery superintendent, stood by. The hole in the wall of the mausoleum also waited. I spoke a few, brief prayers of closure. Joe's family walked away, tearfully. We would regather at their home shortly thereafter for another service, the lighting of the memorial candle, and a shared meal of consolation.

On this occasion, I found myself lingering in the marble hallway. I had so admired this ebullient physician. I was not laying a stranger to rest. His rich voice played in my head—a medley of tunes and tributes. Bart and Pat had exited temporarily as well. I was suddenly alone with the closed casket.

"Well, good-bye, old crooner," I said to the box, turning my back and walking away to my next responsibility. And then, from behind me, and making its way across the plaques and nameplates of the crypted hallway came an unmistakable refrain, sung in a muffled, yet familiar voice:

GA-ry Indi-A-na,
My home sweet home!

I did not look back. I could not. But even as the ephemeral lyric crawled across my skin and tugged at my breath, I only felt happy and reassured inside. It was an agreeable mixture of music and mausoleum that I immediately hoped was also being shared with Dr. Tallisman's family.

While the cemeteries, mausoleums, and memorial chapels that I visit are notable for their essential stillness, this was hardly the first time, professionally or personally, that I have heard from the dead. It is sometimes hard *not* to hear from them; they are always part of our subconscious and conscious thoughts and reveries. Certainly we start with the understanding that in the matter of hearing from the dead, the term "hear" is subjective. My own experience, added to my conditioning as a rabbi, have combined into a sense that our deceased, while physically dead, do influence, guide, and commiserate with us. There may very well be more to our existence than we actually apprehend; the Talmud states: "This world is only the vestibule to another."

Part of the perplexity of our mortality is the fact that, regardless of science, beyond skepticism, and in spite of our understandable and healthy need to separate the living from the dead, we have no way to empirically prove that there is not another dimension to our lives. I don't think that people should dwell on or with the dead, and I certainly affirm that we must accept mortality as the measure of life's limits. But I do not disclaim that we can detect some things from the dead, even as I somehow heard a mausoleum rendition of a stanza from *The Music Man*.

There are some cases that are more extreme than others. It may not be reasonable to accept the testimony of a young convicted murderer from Pennsylvania about his visit from the dead, but that visit certainly proved advantageous to the judicial system. The Associated Press recently reported about Craig Rabinowitz, a suspected murderer and thief, who was directed to come clean by three of his departed loved ones.

Rabinowitz maintained that an intruder had broken into his suburban Philadelphia home and strangled his wife, Stefanie. Rabinowitz was accused of murdering his wife so that he could collect on her insurance policy. The misguided man had accumulated huge debts, including significant funds owed to a lavish strip club. Now, according to press reports, Rabinowitz was pleading guilty after having a dream in which Stefanie and two others appeared to him.

Rabinowitz told a county judge that he was entering the plea because his wife, his father, and his father-in-law visited and spoke to him: "They put their hands on my hand and said, 'Craig, it's time for you to do what's right. It's time for you to do the right thing.'"

None of us can verify that Stefanie and the two fathers actually talked to Craig, but most of us would agree that it was a good thing they did. Craig, meanwhile, was sentenced to life in prison without any possibility of parole. The dead have spoken.

Both the Hebrew Bible and the New Testament contain stories of the dead commingling with the living. Not all of the accounts derive from as baleful a circumstance as the tragic modern case just described; the murderers of the world do not obtain special access to the hereafter. Indeed, some of the biblical episodes, driven by the notion of resurrection, brim with hope. Scripturally, the dead don't necessarily just spook us; they sometimes inspire and direct us.

There can be a useful effect of all this, if the setting and the environment and the purpose are appropriate and genuine. In my role as rabbi, I have listened as some serious and thoughtful people shared their conversations with the dead. "My dad told me what I should do next," one college student advised me. She made some key decisions, fortified by her late father's instruction. It doesn't really matter if her father actually spoke to her in a metaphysical sense. One way or another, he articulated something that was clarifying to his daughter.

I *can* learn something from the dead if I find them in my dreams or discover them through the vestibule of my Bible. Quiet visits at someone's grave can also create understanding and healing. There is nothing wrong or necessarily misguided about talking with a loved one at the site of his or her memorial stone; there are often important things to bestow and receive.

On the other hand, it's not certain how much can be garnered when the dead are "encountered" or "sighted" at a carnival or a mini-mart. Elvis Presley, for example, is no oracle. He is an expired musician whose memory is being exploited by people who respect neither the dead nor the living. In the spectrum of mortality, and in spite of today's entrepreneurs and evangelists, there remains a difference between the holy and the profane. Remembrance and tribute represent one category of interaction with the dead; contrived trysts with the dead represent something else altogether, and frequently amount to a series of burlesque mummeries.

Better that the dead should come to us than that we should pursue them. It is usually more illuminating that way, less forced, and, often enough, less incendiary. Too many crimes have been committed by perpetrators who rationalized their misdeeds based on messages or directives that were supposedly coerced from spirits. When we go after the dead, the living are often hurt. When the dead drift to us, at the cemetery, in church, or in any prayerful moment, the living are sometimes enlightened.

In the First Book of Samuel, the melancholy King Saul pursues the ghost of the prophet. Samuel, who vexed Saul often enough while still living, nonetheless influenced and instructed the troubled monarch. Now, the king's spiritual stock is low, his military fortunes are ebbing, and he desperately wants some insight from the departed Samuel. In a strange twist, Saul disguises himself one night and seeks out a woman who ostensibly contacts the dead. "Bring up Samuel for me," he demands. The king is granted his request when the woman announces: "I see a divine being coming up from the earth."

But the spirit of Samuel is not altogether pleased about being summoned. "Why have you disturbed me and brought me up?" The king would soon be even more agitated than the reluctant ghost because Samuel proceeds to decree a number of dreadful prophecies about Saul's soldierly prospects, his royal lineage, and his very survival. Better that we should permit the dead to come to us—if and when they are meant to—than to disturb them wantonly.

One of the reasons we sometimes believe that we've heard from the dead is our obvious and understandable concern for their safety and whereabouts. I remember that when my father died suddenly in the spring of 1976, my family was naturally grief-stricken, confused, angry, and, above all, lonely. In a flash, we were deprived of my father's direction and his familiar disposition. We would be freshly aggrieved at each subsequent holiday and milestone, when he was absent from his customary and fussy leadership role at home and in the synagogue.

I recall that immediately following his death, I kept wondering where my father was. I was twenty-three years old at the time, recently married, and profoundly affected. It was even harder, however, for my younger brother and sister. Meanwhile, we were all cognizant of and in pain for our still young mother; none of us were prepared for this sudden and brazen intrusion of the mortal facts of life.

But I kept wondering, where is my father now? An answer came from an unlikely source: my uncle, my mother's brother, who arrived from Israel to help us in our sorrow. My Uncle Moshe had never flown in an airplane prior to this quickly organized, merciful mission. To this day, he is not a particularly reverential man. I don't think that he prays very much, and he has suffered much himself, including the sudden loss of his middle boy who died of heart problems some years later. Meanwhile, Moshe has fought in enough of the Middle East wars to make him generally skeptical about human nature.

But my Uncle Moshe, a kind of post-Zionist Tevye the Milkman, does believe in the idea of heaven, and he certainly believed in my father. I asked him, as we walked one night: "Moshe, where is my father?" Moshe thought about it for a moment, wrinkling his brow. Then he said to me: "He's in a good place."

"How do you know that?" I retorted.

"Tell me something." My uncle focused on me. "Your father was very particular, and he didn't have patience for trivialities. If it wasn't a good place, don't you think he'd come back?"

This bit of raw theology has helped me over the years. I understand that Moshe's response amounted to a bit of folk formulation on life and death, but it was very tender and intuitive. He would surely rationalize some things himself about the whereabouts of our dead years later, when his son, Uli, died. Meanwhile, the notion that my father would come back if he was unhappy has continued to give me a measure of comfort and a warm chuckle over the course of time.

But my father himself may have contributed to my sense of well-being about his postmortem situation. Late at night, three weeks after his death, I lay in bed half asleep. A fragrant April breeze floated through the open windows; spring blossoms were emerging following the final frost of March. My wife slumbered peacefully next to me. Now I felt, without a trace of trepidation, that something else flowed in on the breeze.

Looking up toward the ceiling, I saw particles of light swirling above me. It was a most consoling and soothing sight. The light particles, like atoms of intimacy, began to shape themselves into something. I lay and watched, feeling the presence of a commiserating medium. The lights took on a softly luminous silhouette of my father's face—suspended above me and the bed there in the room. I felt no apprehension, only great curiosity and interest.

There was no audible sound, yet I absolutely felt the intonation of words being conveyed to me as the silhouette hovered for a moment. "I am fine, and safe." The words noiselessly penetrated my psyche and warmed my soul. The grains of light dispersed and evaporated. Only the breeze now flowed through the dark room. I was filled with relief and satisfaction. I turned over toward Cathy and fell into a good sleep.

Writing these words now, nearly a quarter-century later, I find no second-guessing occurring in my mind. In the intervening years, I have been with many people who were contemplating, experiencing, or recovering from the loss of loved ones. I am less self-absorbed than I was back then, surely less youthful and naive. I have seen human beings live and die across a wide gamut of mortal experiences. Some have triumphed, others have wisely prioritized, while still others have denied or squandered their mortality. I have taught from the pulpit about the eminence of life, have lamented the devaluation of life that characterizes the digital, postmodern world, and have chastised those who would cynically continue Elvis-style séances with departed celebrities. Life is for living; death is a distinction that should be respected and should instruct our choices and values. And yet: I remember a swirling, private galaxy of lights that came to me with my father's visage and told me not to worry about the other side.

So I was not too skeptical when Kathleen, the upbeat hairdresser mentioned earlier, told me that her mother detects the smell of her late father's cigarette smoke in the house where the parents once shared life. I do not doubt that the dead have departed from us; I'm not sure we can disavow the fingerprints they sometimes leave behind. Nor do I dismiss Kathleen's own report that, in a dream, she dialed her parents' phone number, and after no one answered on the other end of the line, she suddenly awoke with her father's voice, like a clarion, ringing in her ear: *"Hello?"*

Donna Kurit is a freelance writer and editor and a mother who has taken life earnestly, loved her own mother fiercely, and who took her time about getting married. In her late thirties she met Neil, who she felt was the right man, and evidently got a signal from her mother that all boded well.

Some time earlier, Bernice, Donna's mother, had been chatting with her daughter in Rick's Cafe, a pleasant eatery in the suburbs.

Donna was worried about her mother, a gregarious, caring woman who had smoked cigarettes far too long, quit too late, and was falling prey to lung cancer. Bernice was always fretting about Donna's gentlemen callers. On this night, she came up with an unusual criterion for Donna to consider when it came to men: "You ought to see if he ever asks you about your car."

"My car?" Donna was perplexed.

"Yes, your car. It's a practical, daily matter. A man who thinks of such things, especially with respect to his woman, is functional and wonderful. Remember that."

Several months later, after Bernice died, Donna met Neil. While they were having dinner out together, Neil was clearly drawn to the pretty writer with the soft disposition and the sad eyes. Suddenly, Neil asked Donna: "Tell me, have you had your car winterized yet? It's important, and can save you a lot of headaches later."

Donna blinked away her tears of joy. She felt her mother's hand on her shoulder as she looked into her future husband's face—there in Rick's Cafe.

But it was just after Bernice succumbed that Donna really felt her mother's ethereal proximity. A few days after the funeral, Donna went to her mother's apartment—a space the two had shared on many occasions and through many crises, transitions, and milestones. This was the first time Donna would sleep alone in the apartment.

At about 4:00 in the morning, Donna awoke and went into the bathroom. "I felt a sort of cool swirl," she told me. "There was a vague smell of smoke—or something like smoke. I couldn't discern what it was. But I felt my mother in the room with me. I felt her nearby. She was absolutely there. I didn't get scared. I was not upset. It felt right. I felt her essence. There wasn't exactly a sound, but I heard her talking to me. She said, 'This is me. I don't want you to worry. I am here for you. I will always guide you. I will only come to you this one time, but I want you to know that I am always with you.'"

"What happened then?" I asked Donna, vividly remembering my father's swirling silhouette.

"Nothing. It was a wonderful, soothing experience. I just went back to bed, and felt reassured."

Helen Wahba, the gentle radiology nurse with whom we already visited, brings some science to this life/death discussion. Helen thinks a lot about the "out-of-body" experiences that a number of her patients have corroborated. Level-headed, rational, adept, Helen claims no such episode for herself, but she is quietly struck by the clarity and accuracy associated with such reports. She recalled the popular Louisville television personality referred to in the previous chapter, whose heart stopped, and who technically died twenty-eight times in the emergency room. "To complete that story," she told me, "he at some point in time had that out-of-body experience. He told us the next day that he remembered that he was on the ceiling, watching what we were doing. He was able to tell us exactly what had gone on. He had a different perspective from up there, but he was absolutely accurate in his account of the room, the procedures, everything."

Helen added that this was but one of many such experiences to which she was privy, all of them smacking of correctness and sureness. "It has fascinated me," said the nurse who lives in the hard domain of science but hears from the malleable realm of mystification. "It has made a big difference in my outlook."

My folksy uncle, Moshe, who helped with my grief, suffered a terrible loss of his own when his son, Uli, died. My cousin was in his mid-thirties, frolicsome, easygoing, yet susceptible to a congenital vascular defect that had always concerned us. Uli's rather sudden demise was not altogether unexpected, but it was dreadfully unsparing for his wife and his three small children. He was truly a moderate man, soft in tone, and without affectation.

On his last day on earth, Uli actually succumbed twice. He was considered technically dead early in the afternoon, but was miraculously revived by the medical team. He relapsed unconditionally early that evening, even as his family had briefly celebrated the uncanny reprieve. But in between the coda and the curtain, Uli had told a remarkable tale to his hearkening wife.

My cousin said that he had floated above the hospital bed and been drawn to shining, beckoning light. He told his wife that, upon death, he felt a tremendous lift of air under the wings of his body. It was a wondrous sensation, he exclaimed, filled with rapture and deliverance. He then proceeded to a kind of celestial gateway. He was soon greeted by our mutual maternal grandfather, Shmuel—for whom Uli was nicknamed. Uli described the grandfather with details that were precise and familiar to those who had known the patriarch.

There were two aspects to Uli's report that were particularly remarkable. In the first place, my cousin had never been an exceptionally spiritual or religious individual. While I saw him rarely, it was clear that he did not have any defined God-concept, and he would have likely preferred to discuss television over divinity. Beyond that, Uli had never met Grandfather Shmuel. The old man had pre-deceased all of us cousins some fifty years ago. We had only seen worn-out, grainy photographs of him taken in Jewish Palestine. But Uli described the grandfather's features, his gestures, even the timbre of his voice. There was no logical way for Uli to have known as much as he did about the grandfather without having, in some way, visited with him.

When Uli's heart stopped again that evening, he did not return with further testimony about the light and the rendezvous with our grandfather. But in between the two shadows, my simple cousin left us with a report that—aside from our terrible grief—left us feeling our skin against the pounding of our own hearts.

It was but three hours after Cathy's father died that we appeared to hear from him. A series of incidents seemed cloaked in melancholy; the generally accepting cancer victim yielded to a restive spirit. We drove in our car, freshly devastated by the news of Marty's demise. We were hurriedly making plans for the funeral, which would take place the very next day. A bird flew directly into the windshield, dropping helplessly into the street under our wheels. We were at once thrown from our sorrow into ancillary feelings of remorse and foreboding. Why did this eerie thing happen just then?

Cathy is a sensible, extremely centered, amiable woman not given to flights of fancy. A born teacher, she sees things plainly through her green eyes. She laughs heartily when things are funny; she cries intently when times are sorrowful. Marginally superstitious, she believes basically in hard work, day-to-day love, and genuine commitment. When she heard that her father died, she was not looking for falling birds, finicky clocks, or any other peculiar indications. She just wanted to weep and to remember a very nice man who was her champion.

But Marty's grandfather clock would participate in the puzzlement as well. Year upon year until then, the venerable timepiece faithfully chimed on the half-hour. The day after Marty's funeral, the clock decided to ring out at 3:20 in the afternoon. A series of erratic, off-schedule bells continued to mystify us during the memorial week following the funeral, some during the day, some during the night, all ostensibly signaling some kind of restless call from the departed grandfather himself.

There were other strange and notable developments. Cathy had given her father a video- and audio-cassette package on the theme of natural healing during his final weeks. When, a few days after his death, members of the family gathered to watch another, special video that had been prepared in honor of Cathy's parents' recent fiftieth anniversary, it was difficult to insert the videotape into the VCR unit that sat opposite's Marty's venerable reclining chair. Exasperated, someone reached into the video machine and discovered the problem. Inexplicably, the *audio* cassette companion to the prior-mentioned healing video was lodged, inappropriately and mysteriously, into the mouth of the VCR unit. No one could possibly explain this. Meanwhile, a pair of Marty's shoes appeared unceremoniously on the stairway one morning, and a book about natural herbs that had been brought to Columbus for him, and which had not left the shelf, suddenly languished one afternoon on the floor in the middle of the living room.

During his final days, my father-in-law had spoken whimsically about taking a cross-country jaunt, by train, from Ohio to California. Who could blame the ailing man for dreaming of a journey away from himself and from his predicament? We all listened to his yearning with a mixture of understanding and sadness. Then one night, about two weeks after his death, my younger daughter, Debra, a generally reasonable teenager, ran into the house from our backyard. She was quite unsettled as she declared that she had heard a shrill train whistle while making her way toward the house. As we warily opened the back door and peered out, the porch lightbulb suddenly exploded. We were quite relieved that no one was hit by the hot, shattering glass even as we wondered what Marty was so agitated about.

Did it all really happen as we imagined that it did? Was my father-in-law truly engaged in some kind of post-life outreach to his family? I am a serious clergyman with big responsibilities and I tend to believe that he was. Intellectually, it doesn't make much sense; emotionally, it is both portentous and reassuring. In the court of spirituality, I would not testify against it, even if I could concede some circumstantial evidence about displaced shoes, mismanaged cassettes, recalcitrant birds, or ethereal train whistles.

Hope, need, and circumstances can combine into some significant exchanges with the dead. The provenance of such encounters may be in the heaven or it may be in the heart, but what counts is that it just may be. Michael London, the little boy who died in that kibbutz swimming pool, was known to have relished thunderstorms. Why then did a heavy thunderstorm roll into the neighborhood just as we mourners concluded our first prayers of the memorial week and were emerging into what had been, moments before, the bright summer sunshine of the Londons' front yard? "It's Michael," said his bereaved father. Could anybody doubt such an assertion at that moment? Could anybody completely refute it?

Some twenty years ago, I visited a dying man who was an integral part of a synagogue community that I served on Long Island. Abe was avuncular and loquacious, and, in his final weeks, profoundly ill and weakened from cancer. Abe was a structural engineer and, in special service to his congregation, oversaw the building of the synagogue's ceremonial booth each year during the fall harvest festival of *sukkot*. There just wouldn't be a *sukkah*—a little hut—without Abe's supervision and direction that began immediately following the High Holy Days every September or October.

An unusual aspect of the holiday of *sukkot* is its idiosyncratic inter-action with the ancient spirits of the book of Genesis. Many people know that, during the holiday, observant Jews visit or even sleep in the booths, take meals therein, and ritualistically notice the daytime sky or the nocturnal starshine that must be allowed to permeate the deliberately perforated ceiling of the *sukkah*. There is the notion of natural harmony inherent in this, and of humankind's abiding frailty. You are supposed to eschew the building of hard walls, physical and spiritual, during this season of gentle renewal and open spaces. You are also supposed to openly welcome the spirits of the biblical fathers and mothers into one's *sukkah*, even as you pray and apportion meals there. In effect, you are breaking bread and sharing ideas with Abraham, Sarah, Isaac, Rebekah, Jacob, Leah, and Rachel. Some people regard this more literally than others, but there is no question that this amiable holiday has a lot to do with an invitation to, and with hospitality for, departed souls.

When Abe died, his family and friends comforted one another with the sentiment that a *sukkah*-builder was needed in heaven, so God summoned the kindly designer. His wife, Shirley, told me: "I miss him terribly, but that idea really helps me. I'll feel him every time I enter a *sukkah*."

Shirley undoubtedly seeks out Abe's spirit, particularly at the fall holiday. A few years afterward, she told me that she does not com-municate with Abe at his gravesite—a perfectly appropriate and often satisfying environment in which the dead may impart to us. But that is not where it happens for her. "We talk once a year," said Shirley. "It's always in the same place. I smell the leaves and the fruit, and I can hear Abe telling me what to do."

Shirley is not the only one. Hundreds of miles from Abe's original *sukkah* on Long Island, nearly two decades succeeding, I enter an expensively designed *sukkah* that is constructed just outside my temple in suburban Cleveland. I bless the wine and the bread, the little citron called the *etrog*, and the leafy stalks of a green plant called the *lulav*. With congregants standing by, often shivering in the fall wind, I shake the *lulav* in every direction, east, west, north, south, hoping to spread blessing to all the four corners of the earth. The wind draws back, delivering aloft the presence of Abraham, Sarah, Isaac, Rebekah, and the rest of the biblical ancestors. But in most years, I also hear another voice whispering in my ear—a second Abraham. *"Firm up the poles in the northeastern corner of this booth, Rabbi. They're not so steady."* In the *sukkah*, Abe is proximal, friendly, silent, yet audible.

Do the dead tell us things? If we loosen our grip a bit on physics and deduction, they not only speak to us but they sometimes have a lot to say. Dialectically, there is, of course, little to assert here; the dead are dead, and there are no such things as ghosts, mediums, voices, or apparitions. Nor does a gravestone or a memento amount to a talisman. But wherefore the provenance of so many encounters, experiences, out-of-body reports, and images, including some that I myself cannot deny? I don't believe in ghosts but I do believe in souls. The former category is dark, the latter, light. The dead can communicate with us, especially if we allow ourselves to relate to this possibility *spiritually* and not require that it occur cognitively. And even when we know that logically, someone who died could not have actually spoken to us, nonetheless there are instances when, circumstantially, someone indeed does speak to us. There was such a case, born of tragedy, that transpired in New York City several years ago.

"All this for twelve dollars," said Caroline Isenberg, a twenty-three-year-old nighttime robbery and murder victim who was stabbed nine times on the rooftop of her Manhattan apartment building. I worked in New York at the time. The incident, and her words, were reported by the *New York Times* in December of 1984. "I should have given him the money. I should have let him do it. I should have given in." The strange, disorienting thing about the drama for the newspaper-reading and radio-listening public was that when these words came to us in the morning from Caroline, she was already dead. In the case of Miss Isenberg, an aspiring actress who screamed in vain while her life was being snuffed out, hers was a voice that spoke from a dark rooftop, seemingly *after* leaving this world.

Caroline, extroverted, slender, with shoulder-length chestnut hair, was cited in the media as a victim among victims. Her affluent background and distinguished, Northeastern breeding lent her case a certain celebrated status; more than one columnist pointed out in the local press that, because she was a girl of pedigree, her murder (among the 1,500 New York City murders that year) gained Page-One prominence. This was ironic, given that Caroline's violent death converted her into an absolutely equivalent statistic. What was unusual about her, and was a tribute to her intrepidity, was the fact that we honestly thought she was still talking to us hours after she exhaled her last breath.

The attack took place at approximately 1:30 A.M. atop the roof of Caroline's seven-story building on Manhattan's Upper West Side. The assailant, who escaped but was captured several days later, seized the woman off the creaky tenement elevator and forced her to the roof. Caroline's screams and struggle were heard by neighbors; she was so vocal through the nightmare that at one point she even leaned over the ledge and yelled out "929! 929!" to the police officers who had mistakenly gone to the roof next door at street number 925.

The attacker fled as the rescuers approached, and Caroline, bleeding, gasping, clinging to life, began an extended monologue as she was bandaged, injected, wrapped, and evacuated. As the fluids ran through and out of her, she gave a flowing account of the entire incident, even speculating on what she should have done. The culprit had demanded to have sex with her, she said, and she flatly refused. She expressed regret that she had resisted, "for twelve dollars." She described her assailant, thereby giving him a certain grisly humanity. The medical teams thought that Caroline's lucidity indicated that she would survive; she died just after daybreak, from lacerations in her left lung and liver.

The reports of her demise and the remarkable statements she made about her tragedy became so intertwined that it grew difficult to determine which had come first. The young woman touched a deep chord in us because of the sequence: When we woke up that morning, we first learned that she had died. It was then that we began to hear her quoted, recounting everything. Caroline Isenberg's striking final soliloquy roused our deepest feelings about death and dying. She was gone, but she had spoken to us from that nocturnal rooftop—not only about her own situation, but about our collective vulnerability and mortality. I never knew this woman, but I have never forgotten her or the fact that the dead and dying send us important words from a gray area somewhere in between heaven and earth.

I asked Sharon Beckett, the daughter of a fundamentalist minister and the granddaughter of missionaries who once traversed Africa saving natives for Christ, about whether or not the dead speak to the living. Sharon now lives with her husband, Edward, in Altadena, California, adjoining Pasadena. The Becketts are artisans and advertising entrepreneurs; their stately but welcoming home, filled with paintings and computers, sits on a foothill up against the San Gabriel mountains, and it fills up with the scent of the lemon trees that grow in their backyard. It is worlds away from that of Sharon's grandfather, who, she said, "seemed to be forever roaming about East Africa, climbing Mt. Kilimanjaro, discovering gold, going on safari, in between building Sunday schools around the countryside." Sharon, a sensitive, prayerful, completely modern individual, showed me an entry from her grandmother's diary, dated October 4, 1926: *"Today, I realize that my strength is small. . . . The Africans need more than education and civilization. The most to be saved, it is the only remedy."*

What does the grandchild of missionaries think about life beyond death? Sharon's answer struck me as edifying and satisfactory: "I don't see death as anything but a passage into another mode of living. Some kind of life springs from death in every instance that I've known and my meager knowledge of physics leads me to believe that the universe does not *uncreate*." Sharon herself emphasized the last word. She paused to reflect, pulling back her bountiful hair, drawing upon her valued memories.

"I've cradled the lifeless bodies of six of my beloved four-legged pet companions in life. I've handled the cremated remains of my husband's mother, and my favorite uncle. The ashes, bone fragments, and carcasses were but spiritless remains that I symbolically gave back to God. The unresponsive remains that I touched could no longer contain a soul. Life had mutated, or death had caused life as I know it, to metamorphose into something beyond my comprehension, but not beyond my imagination."

Not beyond my imagination. Regardless of science, the aspirations of the human spirt know no boundaries. The only boundary we know, and must acknowledge, is that of physical life. Like Sharon, we all occasionally see, touch, and hold the evidence of former existence. We are wise to acknowledge life's limits, prudent not to vainly pursue or utilize ghosts. That too often amounts less to imagination than to exploitation. But meanwhile, our faith systems all generally venerate the eternity of every human soul.

The body is a shell that we shed, no doubt. The soul exists in its own citadel. There seem to be moments when souls mingle. There is hope in all of this—hope not unrelated to that which has kept dying people alive longer than expected in order to live until somebody's graduation, or for another Yom Kippur, or for one last Christmas. We see these little triumphs and we marvel. Then we move on to life's necessary banalities. But if the soul is the home of optimism, why are we so skeptical that optimism has a home? Why are we so circumspect about imagination, when all we can do to make sense of loss is to imagine? When people have died, we return their bodies to the earth. But why give the earth the soul as well?

The letter was written just a few days before Emma Bennett's death; the writer was her longtime friend Jeanette. Emma and Jeanette had always been frank with each other; it was Emma who especially set the tone for candor. Therefore, the dear ones in her life knew that now, in discussing her impending departure from life, they could and should be direct. "I want so much to tell you 'thank you' for your friendship," Jeanette wrote. "You were my first friend. The fun and good times were many: tennis, Canada, Christmas on Longboat Key, hiding the chocolate fudge from the kids so *we* could eat it, the Chinese restaurant, fish-and-chips, you and Matt at the piano and Jimmy and I asleep (not together!)." Reading the handwritten note, Emma laughed from behind her oxygen mask at the recollection of her playing the piano with Jeanette's husband, Matt, while Jeanette snoozed alongside Emma's Jimmy.

Jeanette knew that Emma was about to die, but the two friends had every intention of retaining a connection. Jeanette wrote: "I shall never hear 'What I Did for Love' without thinking of you—but my eyes won't be dry! You shall live in my heart and be reflected by the good and noble things that you taught me."

Jeanette concluded the warm and forthright letter by informing her dying confidante: "I shall check out the ladies and the casseroles that Jimmy gets and make sure that they're good for him."

Many months later, Jimmy stood over Emma's grave at the Mayfield Cemetery. As usual, it was Friday afternoon; this was Jimmy's weekly ritual enroute to his temple's Sabbath eve service. He was not so well himself, having dealt with two bouts of neck surgery. He wore a brace above his collar, and retained Emma's face in his memory. "I hear from her," he once told me. "I always think about her, and, sometimes, when I stop by the cemetery, I talk to her. She seems to come to me there. I talk to her and I say to her: 'I know you can hear me, so tell me what you think.'"

At Emma's grave one Friday afternoon, Jimmy remembered the trips he took, alongside Emma, to Turkey and Egypt. In Turkey, she documented the work of a group of plastic surgeons and their project with the poverty-stricken and infirm. "You earned five Emmy nominations for that show," Jimmy whispered to his wife in the cemetery.

"We couldn't get any funding for it, though!" Jimmy heard Emma telling him, with a chuckle. *"We did the program for expenses and the experience."*

Jimmy smiled to himself. The sense of his wife's voice flooded his head with vivid memories: There was the helpful driver provided to them by the Turkish ministry of health, and the endless cups of strong Turkish coffee they consumed after the driver delivered them for questioning by uniformed, gun-toting guards in one particular town. Jimmy laughed appreciatively. Neither he nor Emma understood the language or the situation until the guards released them and their obliging driver drove them and their film crew across the countryside to locate and help an ailing teenage boy in need of some surgery.

"What about the madness in Egypt?"

Oh, yes, Jimmy remembered, his stomach tightening a bit. On the very first day, as he and Emma arrived in Cairo, a massive earthquake devastated the city. Hundreds died, and scores of buildings crumbled. The two of them saw things they would never forget. Later, as they visited Aswan, Jimmy remembered how indisposed he suddenly became. Emma took care of him, nursing him through the nightmare of enduring a serious illness in a foreign land. "You taught me how to survive." Jimmy spoke to the headstone in the field. "I know you can hear me. Tell me what you think."

Jimmy, a gentle man with few illusions, receives direction, insight, even admonition, there in the cemetery, at the physical site of Emma's recalled essence. Taken in perspective, received with sanctity, he has what amounts to a useful and meaningful colloquy with the one he loved. Who would want to deny him?

I believe that the dead, in recollection, can and do inform our lives. There are a million visits with the dead, mostly unstructured and informal, that occur daily in every corner of the world. The extent of "discourse" with someone deceased (whatever "discourse" means) may very well be the measure of how much a parent or spouse or friend or mentor actually taught us. There is no way to absolutely disprove that the dead do communicate with us, even as some people carry this notion to extreme or unhealthy lengths.

Somehow, somewhere, there are conversations with the dead. Perhaps the key criterion here is not what we know. It's what we feel. And if what we truly feel gives us a little more peace with mortality, then it amounts to something we know.

Chapter Six

—≈ঔচ≈—

On Talking to the Grieving and the Dying

"I'm sorry that your father passed," I heard a visitor tell a grieving son during a condolence call. It was well intended and genuine, but it lacked the desired effect.

A few moments later, with the earnest visitor out of earshot, the mourner said to me: "What did my father pass? The bar examination? His driver's license test? My father's dead. The fellow could have just told me he's sorry that my father died. He's having a harder time talking about my father than I am."

There are many ways to talk about someone's death, or to describe our overriding mortality. Most people do the best they can. But when somebody else dies, we surely think of our own inevitable death. Phrases such as "passed away," "no longer with us," "been called to God," and the like transmit a message that is cloaked in our own apprehensions. These are gentle euphemisms for the hard truth. They are not harmful, but they do sometimes sound like rationalizations. We are usually pretty straightforward about our bank accounts, yet strangely solicitous about our mortality. The latter is more certain than the former.

I really had a communication challenge when Bill Frankel, a bright but forlorn musician, killed himself in Los Angeles. Even before this tragedy, his aged parents hardly ever left their apartment in Cleveland, because they had never quite recovered from their daughter Susan's suicide several years prior. Two out of their three children—both young adults—ended their lives deliberately. How was I going to tell the Frankels that Bill had replicated Susan's dreadful act?

I received word about Bill from his other sister, Kip, who also lived on the West Coast. Brave, suffering, yet somehow unstopped by this development, Kip expressed one overriding concern to me on the telephone: "Rabbi, you've got to go tell my parents. I can't do it over the phone. I just can't do it at all. Please go let them know, and I'll be home tomorrow."

Coordinating with the Frankels' closest relatives, I worked up enough courage to go over to the apartment house. Several family members would wait in the lobby until I rang down to them. I had called Mr. Frankel before coming over, indicating my desire to stop by for a visit. "Fine, Rabbi," he said, sounding resigned to something. Later the bereaved father would tell me that he had suspected a solicitation on behalf of our temple.

I walked in and sat down. The couple, gray and already weary from life, politely asked me the reason for my appointment. I told them.

"It's about Bill. I'm afraid Bill is dead."

"What?" They both gasped in horror. I leaned forward, kneeling on the ground next to them, and held out one arm in support of each parent.

Mrs. Frankel's eyes rolled in shock. "Billy? Dead? Was it an accident?"

Mr. Frankel seemed to discern what was coming. "No, it wasn't an accident. I'm sorry to say that Bill took his own life. It happened in his apartment in Los Angeles. Kip called me. She's fine. She asked me to come over here and tell you for her. She's flying home right now. I'm so terribly sorry to come and tell you this. You don't deserve this. But Bill is dead."

"Billy?!"

The mother's shriek filled the tiny room. Mr. Frankel nodded at me. He understood. He had been here before.

The mother was inconsolable. "I understand that Susie had to do it. But Billy? Why, Billy, why?" She rocked in pain, falling into her husband's limp arms. I held them both a little longer, then drew back. I was certain that they comprehended. I went to the telephone and called down to the lobby. Soon the apartment filled with family members. People tried to comfort one another. Plans were made. A tortured process began. I eventually withdrew from the scene and went to sit in my car. I struggled to put the key into the ignition slot and realized that my hand was trembling. I felt my throat tightening. I saw Bill's departed sister, Susan, lying in her coffin just a few short years earlier. I gasped for some air. I drove off, satisfied that I had told the Frankels exactly what they had to hear.

When talking about death, we are talking about one of the sure things in life. We should be caring, but not equivocal. We should be gentle, but not indirect, even if the very customs of language seem to blur the realities.

Almost every Saturday morning, a youngster, aged thirteen, comes up to the pulpit of my temple and passes through the ritual of becoming a *bar* or *bat mitzvah*. During the course of the ceremony, the child normally reads and conducts a significant portion of the Sabbath service. For years, I have heard and observed something about these children: Diverse as they may be, they almost each have the same problem with a particular liturgical verse. The line in the prayerbook, occurring in the midst of a responsive reading, is printed as follows:

You are our hope in death as in life.

It is a simple statement about God, coming during the course of the rite known as *"Avot,"* a prayer recalling our ancestors. God has just been praised as the source of life, the support for the fallen, and the author of freedom. Now the reader at the pulpit declares that God is equally our hope in death as in life. But invariably, regularly, notably, the youngster on hand, boy or girl, richer or poorer, extroverted or shy, exuberant or timid, poised or intimidated, reads the line out loud with the following inversion: *"You are our hope in life as in death."*

I have been continuously fascinated by, and sympathetic to, this weekly phenomenon. In what could be described as a kind of emotional dyslexia, the successive teenager is simply unable to put death in front of life—even if it's just a matter of reading a sentence. It is a recurring, small moment that is probably noticed by no one other than myself, but it reveals something about the understandable inability—particularly in a young person—to speak directly about death.

That certainly is not a problem for the people of Oaxaca and Xoxo, in southwestern Mexico. Blending pre-Columbian and Christian traditions, Mexicans gather each year in these neighboring provincial towns to observe *El Dia de los Muertos*—The Day of the Dead. The festival, an official pageant that is actually observed throughout Mexico and by Hispanic communities in the United States and Canada, is historically related to Halloween. It formally begins on October 31, known as All Hallows Eve, and continues through November 1 (All Saints Day) and November 2 (All Souls Day). According to Guy Garcia, a self-described "second-generation California Chicano" who was raised in the suburbs, the fiesta represents both a vivid visit with his past as well as a straight dialogue with and among the grieving, the remembering, and the dead.

Writing recently in *Sky* magazine, Garcia declared that "the mystical rites of the ancient Aztecs, Mayas, and Zapotees are more than exotic curiosities; they are living windows into a realm that seems light-years away from my life in the United States, where magic has succumbed to the cold reason of science, and ghosts are relegated to movies and the pages of gothic novels." Garcia stressed that the strange, wondrous carnival, replete with candle-laden graves, papier-mâché skeletons, salsa musicians dressed as corpses, marigolds, incense, chocolates, nuts, fruits, fireworks, and miniature skull candies, is ultimately intended to ease the tension between the living and the dead. Visitors to the festival, most of whom come from the United States, have been affected by the unreserved expressions of both grief and revelry, when, in Garcia's words, "mourning becomes a public act." While eating *pan de muertos* (the bread of the dead), or building little altars for the returning *angelitos* (souls of dead children), a person no longer has any difficulty organizing a thought or a sentence juxtaposing death and life. A bit surreal, even macabre, The

Day of the Dead nonetheless removes the exigency from the discussion of death, even endowing it with a certain normalcy.

A reporter for National Public Radio went to Oaxaca on assignment during the festival in 1993, shortly after losing her mother. Vertamae Grosvenor spoke about it, and about a subsequent visit taken with her grandson, during a more recent NPR broadcast. Concerning her first visit, Grosvenor said: "Death was everywhere in Oaxaca. It was impossible to avoid a direct confrontation. And yet, I came away comforted."

The second visit came in the aftermath of the sudden death, by car crash, of Ms. Grosvenor's son-in-law, Bo. A drunken driver had swerved into and killed the musician, leaving eight-year-old Oscar without a father. Vertamae could not find the words to explain this calamity to the child. Nor is our culture altogether comfortable with the challenge of talking to the grieving about the dead. So Vertamae remembered the unusual but solacing pageant in the southwestern pueblo, and she took Oscar for a journey to Mexico.

Ms. Grosvenor is descended from the Gullah peoples of the Sea Islands, an African grouping that has inhabited the coastal areas of South Carolina, Georgia, and northern Florida. She was intrigued by the comfortable Mexican interaction with the dead because of her heritage people's custom of referring to a funeral as a "home going." In Oaxaca, she and her grandson noted the ongoing family reunions centering around graves and monuments, the easeful sharing and communing. She and little Oscar were able to open up to each other about their mournful feelings. It became much less arduous to talk to each other, especially about death and mortality.

On the NPR broadcast, Oscar is heard to say about the people he met and observed at Oaxaca: "They're feeling what I'm feeling, but in a different way, because somebody else died in their family. And I think they're under a lot of stress, too. So, here everybody is even." Vertamae Grosvenor said: "We left Oaxaca without answers, but we came away comforted."

There is no question that a key to coping with mortality is not to run away from the subject. This does not always mean that it is necessary to talk. There are times for talking, times for silence, and times for reflection. But there is never a good time to thrust the topic away, because it is certainly the most affecting and experienced circumstance under the sun, and it surely—as Oscar declared—makes everyone "even."

A passage in *Gates of Prayer*, a prayer book of Reform Judaism, has always made sense to me:

> The Psalmist said that in his affliction he learned the law of God. And in truth, grief is a great teacher, when it sends us back to serve and bless the living. We learn how to counsel and comfort those who, like ourselves, are bowed with sorrow. We learn when to keep silence in their presence, and a word will assure them of our love and concern.

It is not easy to discuss their situation with the dying, nor is it easy to discuss their sorrow with the grieving. A lot of this has to do with our own reluctance to acknowledge mortality. Few of us will ever get to The Day of the Dead in Mexico, but all of us will go through those days leading to death, either our own or someone else's.

Generally, it's when we approach adolescence that we begin to think a great deal about death and dying. In spite of the Elvis syndrome of perpetual resurrection that brings back celebrities via CD-ROM and computer-transposed imagery, and in spite of the sense that the dead may communicate with us from beyond this dimension, it is incumbent upon us to make young people realize that death is physically final. There are no absolute guidelines to follow here; a lot of what you say and do falls back upon honest and good instincts. Children certainly know about death; they see it, magnified, exemplified, even glorified a hundred times a week on TV. We should be fairly straight with kids, and not patronize them with euphemisms such as "Grandfather went to sleep." Grandfather did not go to sleep; from sleep Grandfather would arise. When someone in a child's life dies, it is more helpful to attest—with tenderness and patience—that the loved one is now physically gone, even if we assert that he or she has gone on to paradise. No matter how we phrase it, we should certainly indicate to a youngster that the loss is permanent and that the person who died is now beyond our reach and will not return as we remember him or her.

This, again, is why I am so concerned about the mass media's penchant for keeping departed celebrities animated. If Elvis lives, or if John Lennon's voice can be reincarnated by electronic magic on a new Beatles compact disc, then maybe these two victims—one of self-abuse, the other of murder—aren't really dead. The message this sends to impressionable young people is that death is not necessarily final and that fatal practices do not necessarily cause a penalty. Even Nat King Cole's posthumous music video duet with his daughter Natalie concerns me as a confusing, misleading, if mellifluous adventure.

I am worried about all of this because I know that most youngsters as well as adults have enough of a hard time with their awareness and discussion of mortality. Making it seem as though death is not conclusive may bring in profits for entertainment lawyers, estate experts, and copyright specialists. It is not so profitable for young people, who know very little about royalties but a lot about night terror, and who are coping with helpless, even suicidal feelings.

Most adolescents carry or express the sentiment, from time to time, of wanting to die. We know that this is an aspect of growth and development. On one level this is an effect of realizing, for the first time, that death is real and inevitable. Sometime during childhood, a person is suddenly filled with the quiet dread: I am going to die someday! A particularly tender and simple layer of childhood is ripped away. Most every adult can remember, more or less, when this happened to him or her.

One of the ironies for me, as a spiritual leader, is the role that organized religion sometimes plays in this personal drama. It is not always a helpful role, even while having some kind of personal faith is almost always helpful in reconciling mortality. But there is a great deal of morbid interest that can be found in much of organized religion, and this has to be evaluated carefully in our discussions about death.

Some theological leaders point to death routinely, making it a lightning rod for their expressed persuasions. Death is a punishment, or a reward, or both. Martyrdom is ingrained into much of holy writ. A lot of bad folks die, but many good folks die in supposedly enlightening moral scenarios. Death is not infrequently the noble conclusion; for Christianity, the death of its beacon hero is the magnificent crucible that started civilization all over again.

I have no quarrel with anybody's religious faith, and I emphatically believe deeply in what a healthy spirituality can bring to anybody at any time. But I do have a quarrel with any situation that might exacerbate a youngster's already complicated relationship with the idea of death. We should talk to children as openly as possible about mortality, never twisting it with threatening notions of satanic implications transferred from some extravagant pulpit, nor trivializing it with attractions such as freeze-dried "Elvis sweat" transferred from the tabloids.

Years ago, a colleague of mine and his family had a dreadful experience during a family holiday. Michael Cook was driving home to Cincinnati from Toronto, Canada, accompanied by his wife, his three young children, and their seventeen-year-old baby-sitter, Linda. Linda, cheerful, outwardly healthy, had been part of the Cook household for several years. "She had never been outside of Ohio in all her years," said Michael. "This was special." The teenager was particularly helpful to the rabbi and his family because, being Catholic, she was often available to assist them during Jewish holidays and milestones.

After a few days in Toronto, the group began the trek home. At Lake City, Ohio, south of Cleveland, they took two rooms in a motel so that they could spend a day at Sea World. "She had a glorious time," Michael recalled, although during the course of the day, Linda began to complain of a dull headache.

That night, she seemed to drag, and was uncharacteristically unresponsive to the playful children in the room she shared with them. Michael and his wife began to grow anxious about their baby-sitter's pasty complexion and poor disposition. "Only the next morning," said Michael, "did I judge from her wooziness that more than a headache was involved."

It was now evident that Linda was in need of immediate medical attention. "I called an ambulance to the motel, and while it was on its way, I called Linda's parents in Cincinnati. I told them I thought they should come right up. They assured me it was just a headache, but I insisted that they come up."

Trailing the ambulance at speeds of up to eighty miles per hour, Michael felt his heart pounding with alarm and trepidation, while back at the motel, his family fell into a fearful stillness. At the Akron hospital, Linda, now cataleptic, was carted through the emergency room entrance.

Michael correctly suspected an aneurysm as he paced in the alien, austere waiting room. He felt an alarming sense of uselessness. "No, she's not my daughter," the rabbi explained to the inquiring hospital personnel. Nor could he provide any medical history, or any context whatsoever to help explain this nightmare to the white-clad clinical staff into whom he had delivered this unfortunate young woman who took care of his children.

"I felt terribly guilty and embarrassed by what happened, as if it were my fault. Actually, the physicians said that the aneurysm was congenital and might have burst in her brain at the same day and time no matter where she had been. Of course, I also worried what effect this would have on my children, and their potential fears of death. After all, they spent the night with a dying girl, only no one knew it. But the most difficult part of this thing was to greet Linda's parents as they arrived in the hospital there in Akron and tell them that she had died."

Michael Cook, a rabbi, a scholar, but above all a father, was devastated. "I kept thinking that this lovely girl had never even left the state of Ohio before this trip. I rationalized that at least we gave her the happiest trip of her life." But Professor Cook has never been able to set foot in a Sea World park again.

Meanwhile, the rationalization concerning the teenager's death continued more formally in the environs of her church. Michael remembered that at the girl's funeral, there was a sense of "rejoicing" that the teenager was now with Jesus. "It was as if everyone was in denial. The news came shortly thereafter that Linda's sister was pregnant not with one baby but with twins. The parents rationalized that God was giving them another child back in lieu of Linda."

Again, I have no argument with anybody's religious faith, and I certainly am relieved to know when even a rationalization such as the one recalled by Rabbi Cook renders anyone some short-term comfort or explanation. Nobody in the world other than Linda's parents could have known what they were feeling at the time of their inexplicable loss. Yet, according to Michael Cook, who teaches the New Testament to rabbinic and graduate students, Linda's parents *had* gone to their priest seeking some tangible explanation for their tragedy.

Linda's parents had asked Michael to accompany them as they visited the rectory in the immediate aftermath of the death. They poured their heart out to their clergyman and evidently asked the most basic and understandable question that a parent would ask at such an unthinkable time: Where was God when this happened?

"Where were you when Jesus died on the cross?" the priest responded with a studied and practiced bit of his theology.

Assignment of this well of grief into the hands of a deity may very well be a proven and traditional method of religious procedure. It is certainly not confined to Catholic practice—a practice and a liturgy filled with compassion and insight. That particular priest did not represent the finest level of ministerial empathy. I recall an incident that occurred several years ago in Ma'alot, a town in northern Israel. After Arab terrorists murdered twenty Israeli teenagers during an assault on a high school, a fundamentalist rabbi came and announced that the whole episode transpired because the school did not have its *mezuzah* (a container bearing liturgical parchment) properly mounted in its doorway. In the matter of mortality, organized religions sometimes proffer up wide volleys of theological justification when people need specific, directed doses of sympathy and understanding. Meanwhile, Michael Cook did not seem to believe that the retort to Linda's parents helped them deal with the practical reality that lay before them. Nonetheless, the mourning process proceeded for Linda, although it seemed to have more to do with something lofty in heaven than with the ghastly business on earth.

Rabbi Cook had his own children to deal with during this distressing ordeal. When we wish to learn about how to talk to children at such a time, we can ask someone who has been in this position. Linda, after all, was the baby-sitter to three impressionable children—David, Ben and Maia—who were, respectively, eleven, eight, and four years of age at the time.

"I stressed to them that nothing they did had caused this," Michael told me. The father instinctively felt that the kids might bear some guilt. This, in fact, can be a bigger problem for young people than having their own sensations of vulnerability heightened at such a crisis—although the latter is not uncommon, either. "I told my children that they hadn't misbehaved, that they hadn't tired Linda out, and that they hadn't kept her from sleeping. I wanted them not to feel responsible for Linda's death."

Cook anticipated his children's possible anxieties about this disaster, and he spoke plainly and directly to them. He explained to them that the doctors made it clear that their baby-sitter had been very sick before the trip to Canada and Sea World even started. He emphasized to them that she would have died even if she hadn't left home, and he asked them to remember how much she enjoyed the outing. "I also stressed that not one of the three of them was sick like that."

The rabbi did not digress into major theological philosophy with his young offspring. Children generally need death explained to them in down-to-earth terms, although there is nothing wrong in expressing the hope that every person has a soul given by God which then returns to God. Children are not as much in need of detailed speculation as we may think; they are much more in need of our encouragement and our ability to listen. I thought that Rabbi Cook was sensible and intuitive with his kids. He said: "I also told them that we had taken many photographs of Linda, that we would develop them, and that we would still have a little bit of her with us in that way. We would make sure to keep a framed picture of her on our living room mantel."

When someone dies, especially when a child dies, parents and grandparents and others immediately begin to suffer grievously.

What they ought to hear from others should not include guilt-suffused metaphors, but clear and genuine expressions of support. Not infrequently, silence is preferable. People don't always have to hear every word of what you feel; your presence alone can tell them a great deal. Sometimes you may ask yourself, what can really be said that matches the enormity of the situation? There are no formulas or gimmicks and there are certainly no guaranteed ecclesiastical ploys. Maybe Jesus or God or Providence wanted a child. But no one ever wanted a child more than its parents.

A different dilemma that confronts us regarding the language of mortality is the question of why people sometimes feel like they want to die. One reason, already suggested, is that society no longer treats death with the respect it deserves. It seems that some Hollywood moguls, some magazine editors, and even some preachers, have forgotten what their own trembling was like when, at the age of twelve or thirteen, they suddenly realized that life will end someday and that the end of the discussion is nothing but the grave. So, again, parents who brought children into mortal being must consider our own responsibilities to their struggle with mortality. This may not always mean a trip to Oaxaca, Mexico, but a trip to a child's room from time to time, just to talk things over, is hardly ever a wasted effort.

The impact of commercialism notwithstanding, one reason that people sometimes feel like dying is that we put too much pressure on each other. In the case of a young person, a good report card is a worthy goal, but is it really more important than your child's own feelings of worth? When children believe that they can't live up to something, they sometimes choose to simply die. I know—I have buried suicidal children who had everything but their parents' tenderness.

In this matter of suicide, a swelling epidemic in North America, we need to remember that people have always contemplated and been intrigued with it. But today the world is one big video manual showing you how to do it—or how to murder somebody else. Instead of criticizing somebody too much, we ought to listen for signs of self-hatred. Moodiness, angry eruptions, evasiveness, brazenness—all could imply something serious. An obsession with someone, especially someone dead, is deserving of our attention. We mustn't stand on ceremony with the ones we love; better to look out for them now, before we find ourselves standing on their graves.

When fourteen-year-old Jenna swallowed an entire bottle of Tylenol several years ago, severely poisoning her liver, I went to her bedside and prayed. Miraculously, she survived. (Some would assert it's because she was prayed for; maybe so, but I've also prayed to God many times for the strength to understand why someone *hadn't* survived.) When I was finally able to ask Jenna why she had attempted suicide, I wasn't surprised by her answer: "I can't do enough things well."

Here was a child who was a gourmet cook, a gifted flutist, and an accomplished gymnast. Her parents, who had announced their divorce just prior to their daughter's suicide attempt, were also exceptionally talented and brilliant people. But they had forgotten to do one thing: listen to their only child. A lot had been achieved in that well-appointed home, except the one thing that is most important.

It is a fact that young people, in the normal course of events, when confronting mortality, consider death. This is a delicate rite of passage. Meanwhile, our celluloid culture is already soft-pedaling or even exalting the idea of death. We must talk to children about death quietly, in earnest—not only in the aftermath of a death, but especially in the aftermath of one. And when we bring religion into it, it's still important not to leave out the truth.

It should also be remembered that young children and teenagers have varying degrees of awareness about life and death. Some of that, obviously, has to do with personal experience. When I discussed these issues one evening with my Confirmation class of tenth-graders, I heard many echoes of biographical insight.

Sasha, a musical child with delicate intonations, had experienced the deaths of two young acquaintances during the previous few months. There was clearly a feeling of incongruity coming from her about such implausible events. Meanwhile, Sasha enjoyed a great-grandmother who was 102 years old at the time of our dialogue.

Sasha's father had shared a story with me, in fact, about a recent visit the family made to the matriarch. The nursing facility had phoned and suggested that the old woman was finally near the end. The children and grandchildren ought to come over, with some dispatch.

The family hastily arrived at the home. They did not know that, in the interim, the great-grandmother had been rejuvenated and was lying calmly in her bed. Warily, Sasha's parents tip-toed into the room. The old lady looked up, genuinely concerned, and asked: "So, who died?"

Now in class, Sasha was wondering: Why do young kids die, and my relative lives on at 102? "I think it's all a matter of predestination," she told the other youngsters in the class, her voice laden with certainty. Life had truly tested her, and she was thinking things through. "You die when you're supposed to die, whenever that time is, and whatever your age happens to be."

A number of the other students disagreed with Sasha. The debate was urgent and beneficial, I thought. A fifteen-year-old child growing up in America at the millennium cannot afford to be noncommittal about life and death. "If it's all predestination," said Alexis, whose father died two years before, "then nobody has any responsibility for their actions."

"Yeah—why be good?" Someone else chimed in. "If it's all just scheduled to happen, then I can do all this evil, maybe even kill somebody, and then when the court tells me I was guilty, I can just tell them it was destined to happen!"

"People *can* make choices about their health, their diet, their lifestyle," added Alexis. I did not happen to know all the circumstances concerning her father's death, but it was evident that she was a child who had grown immensely from the experience and was now speaking from her point of view with as much conviction as Sasha was from hers.

The dialogue swirled. For the most part, the students who had been blessed so far with uneventful lives were less animated. They were reticent, anxious, somewhat bemused. I was happy for their innocence, hoping it would continue, yet not betray them when life would leaven that innocence. In all, the class was split about predestination, but united in the sentiment that mortality is an equalizing and looming topic in their lives. "We never talk about it at home," said one of them. That bothered me, because virtually any child surely wants to explore this issue with the ones he or she loves most in the world.

"We can't help but talk about it," said Vanessa. The class drew still. Vanessa was wearing a wig; she was recovering from a difficult bout with leukemia. I was well acquainted with her situation and was grateful for her willingness to talk. There was general awareness among the class of thirty-five that Vanessa had already endured an ongoing series of chemotherapy treatments, intermittent hospital stays, and almost intolerable afflictions as a result of her disease. Coping with mortality was not an abstract matter for this congenial, cognizant teenager who could speak with authority about life's priorities.

"I certainly didn't want to get sick," Vanessa said, looking straight at the others. "But it's amazing how close it's made my family. I feel such love from them. It's given me a lot of strength. When you get sick, especially if you're young, you sort of find out what's important."

The confirmands listened. They learned more in that brief moment than I could have ever taught them. And all they did was talk, plainly and simply, without guile and formulas, about the fact that even the most nimble bodies, brimming with adolescence and self-absorption, are nonetheless subject to the nuances of life, informed by discourse, bolstered by the love of others.

In the corner of the room, one young man sat unmoving, his eyes filling with tears. Johnny had lost his aunt to murder just a few years before. A roving killer had entered the store where the young woman worked and brutally ended her life. I wondered if the discussion had been too much for him. Perhaps I should have considered his sensibilities before pursuing this theme in class, or at least forewarned him. He and his family had suffered terribly.

"Are you okay?" I walked over to the tormented lad as the session wound down. Hard memories flooded his face. His fallen, stained countenance told me, again, that sometimes there are no words.

Sometimes you just sit by a person and listen—even if it's just to the fall of rain.

What do we say to a person who has suffered the loss of a loved one? Before we say anything, we need to discern what is happening to such a person, and put it all into a rational context. It is as natural for any person to grieve as it was necessary for that person to draw his or her first breath at birth. An old tome, the Bible, seems to impart some level of comfort to people who need to express emotions at the milestone of bereavement.

In the Book of Genesis, there is the tender account of the death of Sarah, the wife of Abraham. The old couple had traveled a long road together, starting out in Mesopotamia and finishing in Canaan, where they made a covenant with God, converted to a new faith, and parented the idea of monotheism. They also became the parents, at an advanced age, of their one shared child, Isaac. In the twenty-third chapter of the book, we learn that Sarah's life comes to its end: "And Sarah died in Kiryat-Arba—now Hebron—in the land of Canaan. And Abraham came to mourn for Sarah and to cry for her."

And Abraham came to mourn for Sarah and to cry for her. This report is the consummation of one of the earliest obituaries ever recorded in western history. In lean, direct prose, the Bible conveys that the matriarch died, and it specifies where she died. But then, in more swollen, emotional terms, the normally terse Scripture signals to us that when you lose someone you love, you are supposed to go through a process of grieving, *and you are supposed to cry*. Stoicism may have its place, but when you bury somebody who has been a part of you for so long—Sarah was a part of Abraham for decades—you are not expected to be reticent in your expression of anguish and regret. What Abraham was feeling at that critical moment, and what the canon acknowledges so openly, is as biblical as it is current for every one of us who has ever loved somebody.

So the first thing to know when visiting someone in grief is that he or she needs to bewail their dead. Suggestions to the bereaved about how to "cheer up" or to "think of something else" are usually trite and gratuitous. They even potentially demean the situation.

People in mourning are wounded; they must heal in time, and they should not be called to task in the first several days of fresh grief about weeping and wailing. The story of Abraham's sorrow also reveals that men are not precluded from the therapy of tears when experiencing pain. If the visitor cannot handle this, he or she might quietly withdraw, and find some other way to express support and concern.

Rationalizations are risky when trying to encourage mourners. When I spoke to a woman whose adult daughter had lost a premature baby, I offered that "maybe it wasn't meant to be." This was a mistake that caused the grandmother more heartache than consolation. "Don't say that, Rabbi," admonished the sorrowing woman. "It doesn't help when people say things like that. It *was* meant to be. My daughter gave birth to a real person who had a name. Don't say that."

I had unwittingly belittled this grandmother's woe, as well as her maternal agony for her daughter, the bereft mother of the lost infant. My remark had been well meaning, intended to suggest that perhaps the family was spared the long-term traumas that do often afflict surviving premature babies. But, at that moment, in that context, it was a statement that hurt more than it helped. It would have been better to listen a little longer before offering my evaluation. I would have known more. I would have spoken more usefully, even if I had ultimately spoken less.

What people in distress usually want is not an assessment, but an acknowledgment of their situation. Traditional Jews often greet those in mourning with a simple formula: "May you be comforted among the mourners in Zion." Tradition, simplicity, and empathy are compressed into such an ancestral expression of understanding. It bypasses all the small talk, and helps create a format for the speaker who might otherwise meander verbally. It's not always what you say; it's what you evidently feel that really matters to a person whose plight is sometimes too much for words, anyway.

As already suggested in this chapter, I think that few cultures are as uninhibited and forthright about death and mourning as the Hispanic culture. Mexico's Day of the Dead is an overt demonstration of this; one Spanish observer suggested that the overwhelming number of visitors to the death festival are American because, when it comes to the issue of mortality, Americans are "spiritually impoverished."

Over the years, many Mexican-Americans have traditionally formed self-help associations for funerals. When a member of the association died, the others were assessed for the costs of the service and burial. There was no cramped talk about the ritual; it was taken care of with dignity and charity. A study of New York–area Puerto Ricans revealed that a wake may continue for several days, primarily because it is understood that it may take some time before bereaved relatives can properly express their feelings of loss. Meanwhile, in the Puerto Rican culture, it is strongly prohibited to talk wantonly or without respect about a person who has died throughout the initial period of remembrance. Mexicans often stay at the freshly dug grave until the body is lowered into the ground—a practice interestingly similar to that of traditional Jews.

Hispanic people tend to observe extended periods of mourning, wearing black, visiting the cemetery often, and coming to terms without acceding to the brisk, post-modern culture that has compressed so many of life's critical moments. As a rabbi, I heartily endorse the psychologically redeeming aspects of many Jewish mourning rituals. I do think that the deceased should be laid to rest with reasonable dispatch, and I do believe that public viewing of bodies can be invasive of privacy and decorum. While celebrating the inherent wisdom of the Jewish practice of sitting *shiva*, which brings people to the grieving house in order to comfort, reminisce, and share prayers, I nevertheless lament the emotional deflation that has been forced upon this memorial week by the vagaries of our commuter culture and by the lack of patience and honor that people accord to nature's clock. The irony is that the word *shiva* actually means "seven"; these days, it's unusual to see a bereaved family observe a *shiva* that even fulfills three days of dedicated reflection, respect, and healing. Moreover, there is an ominous rise in the number of funeral services that are followed by the declaration of "no visitation." How can you even say anything to a family when the community is barred from visiting and expressing sympathy altogether?

Meanwhile, what do you say when you have the opportunity to speak with someone who has suffered a death? Whatever words you choose, you simply convey that you understand and perceive what he or she is feeling. If you have suffered similarly, your tone—or your careful choice of words—will help the other person to know "I've been where you are." Here again, the Hispanic tradition brings insight: An expression typically heard that is both succinct and sufficient is *"Siento mucho su perdida"*—"I feel your loss very much."

On the other hand, there are times when it can be unbefitting to tell someone that you know exactly how he or she feels. Their circumstances may not at all match any circumstances that you have ever faced. Confronted with the family of my student, Johnny, I would have been hard pressed to suggest that I really knew precisely how they felt when Johnny's aunt was murdered. Quoted recently in *Good Housekeeping*, the bereavement specialist Rabbi Earl A. Grollman made the following cogent point: "I worked with people who'd lost loved ones in Oklahoma City after the bombing. But then, unlike them, I got to go home to my family." Grollman astutely maintains that there are times when "we have to learn to tell the grief-sticken 'I *don't* know how you feel.' "

I recall two exchanges that occurred during the memorial week following my father's death in 1976. One was terribly distracting, the other remarkably kind and uplifting.

As previously shared, my father died suddenly and unexpectedly, playing handball at the local community center. He was generally hailed as vital and robust; there was considerable shock and disbelief among his family and friends. The house filled up with visitors after the burial, which took place within twenty-four hours of the fatal heart attack. Most of the guests were truly shaken, concerned, considerate, and helpful to my mother and her three children. Not a lot of talking went on; the long interludes of silence in the crowded house said everything.

On the second or third day, a gentleman appeared whom we marginally knew. I doubted that he was actually personally familiar with my father; there are some people who seem to regularly appear at houses of mourning, some for the food, some out of curiosity. This man's connections to our family were dubious. The only thing we really had in common with him was that he also frequented the Jewish Community Center. He entered and sat down in the living room during a lull in the throng. My mother, brother, sister, and I sat on mourner's chairs across from him, our black ribbons clinging to our clothing, our hearts broken beneath the clothing.

"So," the man asked presumptuously, "what actually happened to your dad?"

None of us could or wanted to answer. The unwelcome guest was sending us right back to the beginning of our bewilderment. His inquiry was selfish, unfeeling, and unsettling. I eventually attempted to answer politely: "He had a heart attack at the Center." I formed the words in my mouth but they never quite emerged. It was too bizarre a moment. I could not distinguish between my fresh pain that resulted from the question and my indignation that it was even asked. Fortunately for us and the tiresome man, another visitor deftly and discreetly whisked him out the door, complete with a little plate of pastry and fruit.

The next night, it was very warm in the house. The general shock had begun to give way to a watery, aching realization that this was not a bad dream. Sometimes, the hardest days are a few days after a death; the initial numbness begins to disintegrate as the commotion of the funeral, the tributes, the gatherings, and the outpourings yield to the realization that somebody's place is empty and that he or she is just not coming back.

The house was again full, and my heart longed for the more familiar faces of *my own* friends and classmates. Most of the visitors were my mother's peers; their faces were wrinkled with worry, their speech was slanted with exotic dialects, their breath was strong with garlic and coffee. My elusive friend Jack Bluestein had come and gone; he was not good at this sort of thing, and it was better for me to be relieved of his awkward sentimentality. Little did I know that Jack himself would die fourteen years later at an age just five years younger than my relatively young departed father.

Now came a small group of classmates from the local rabbinical school where I was enrolled. I looked up gratefully at my sympathetic friend Cary. Cary, a short, lanky man who prays hard and plays the banjo, hails from Texas, and once strummed for a Jewish cowboy rock band. He stood before me as I sat weeping on the mourner's stool. The familiar faces brought a wave of uncontrollable and necessary heaves. Cary didn't say a word. He took his bare hand and, with a motion as gentle as that of an angel, wiped the sweat off my brow, and the tears off my cheek. It was an act of complete kindness, borne on simpatico wings, that I have never forgotten. He had spoken with his eyes, and made me feel momentarily stronger.

My friends prayed the evening service with us. It was the act of drawing us into a circle of accustomed devotions and chants that soothed and comforted us that sweltering evening. They did not linger—another practical measure that visitors to a house of mourning ought to consider. As with most things, instincts will tell you what to say or not to say, when to come and when to leave. If your considerations are focused not on yourself but on the others—the ones in trouble—you are likely to do and say the right thing. And it is always right to simply listen.

In the end, it is a good experience for just about anybody to visit with and comfort the bereaved. The people least prepared for the eventuality of death are the ones who are rarely or never exposed to the rites of mortality. "I can't go over there," some people will say. "It's too upsetting. I can't deal with it." So often, those who have suffered a loss will tell me in the aftermath: "I found out who my friends really are. Some people really surprised me by being there. Others really surprised me by never showing up or even dropping a line."

Many of us don't "go over there" because we genuinely dread the environment of a grieving household. We can't always know or imagine the pain we sometimes cause by our absence. But it is a worthwhile experience to visit and show respect; one generally grows and gains insight and satisfaction through such a sojourn. Jews regard it as a *mitzvah*—a good deed. Christians exalt it as mercy. It is an act of charity and revelation that salves the hearts of both giver and receiver. It helps you make peace with your own mortality. As the Mexican community seems to discern so well, it is an essential transaction of community because, at the end of the day, we are all "going over there."

And what do we say to a person who is dying?

The first thing to remember is that a person who is dying is also a person who is living. He still wants to be himself, she still wants to take part, as much as possible, in what's going on around her. Most terminally ill people I've met did not appreciate being denied any sense of control over the rest of their lives. They treated their destiny with pretty much the same resources and personality traits that they always had manifested: If someone was funny, he tended to use humor at this stage, as well. Highly organized people remained fairly meticulous, planning their own funerals, filing ethical wills, managing the insurance and financial paperwork, coordinating a variety of family issues. Unless, of course, the medical protocol itself was changing the chemistry of the situation (and this certainly happens often enough), a person who was busy and demanding throughout her life was not going to suddenly surrender her disposition at this most critical stage. Nor was a leader necessarily planning now to simply follow, even as a self-centered individual was not likely going to convert to magnanimity.

When my father-in-law was in the throes of his final months (the cancer had metastasized from his esophagus to his liver), my sister-in-law was caught in an especially trying predicament. Elena, the single mother of two young boys, had been living for several years in Australia. Ironically, she was making plans to return to Ohio just as her father's condition became apparent. But most of the information and the news about Marty was exchanged with us via electronic mail. The news was not getting better, and Elena was having a hard time coping.

She found herself disconnected, physically and spiritually, from the crisis. While Elena regarded her imminent return home with an intense mixture of uneasiness and relief, she also felt a discomfiting blend of grief, rage, sorrow, and helplessness. After some thirty years of wandering about the globe, she knew that she was coming home this time to see her father die. She wanted to make up for a lot of lost time and misplaced emotions; there wasn't going to be much time.

Her e-mail postings to Cathy and me were filled with nostalgia, homesickness, and remorse. Tormented by feelings of flux and uncertainty, Elena shared her regrets about failed marriages, unfulfilled dreams, and difficult financial straits. She appeared to be trying to get her ailing dad to forgive her for what she now perceived as her forfeited years, dating back to her college days at Berkeley and elsewhere. She wondered to herself if he was truly pleased with her (he unequivocally was, and loved her unconditionally); if he knew, behind the cancer veil, that she adored him and longed for his approbation.

I thought that it was all understandable and genuine anguish, but that it was perhaps being misfired at the dying man. Elena was in a terrible emotional dilemma, and was looking for a place to alight. Trying to suggest or even make decisions for her father and mother from halfway around the world, while carrying so much emotional baggage, would prove futile.

Four months before Marty died, I sent an e-mail to Elena in Australia: "You can't do much else than wrap your arms around your boys, collect your things, hold your head up, and make your way through your journey," I suggested. "Nor can we force a plan on a developing and fragile situation. We'll see what your mom wants, when such a time comes. We'll also first see what your father does with the remainder of his life, and learn from him what thoughts he has about your mother's future. He is not done being a husband, a father, a grandfather, a good friend."

I knew I was being a bit tough on my warmhearted sister-in-law, but I also knew, from being on the scene with Cathy, that Marty did not want the rest of us to tell him what to do (even while we necessarily manipulated some things quietly to advance his welfare). I added to Elena: "I also submit to you, respectfully, that *his* feelings, sensibilities, and comfort are the issues right now. This is not really about our collective middle age, being sandwiched between the generations, coping with memories of relationships with parents, etc. All these issues surely resonate, but the focus is on your dad, not any of us. Again, we need to listen to him, attend to him, and, of course help him as we can—leaving our own angst and reflections on how life has treated us, or how we took this course or that, somewhat out of the picture, especially *his* picture."

I imagined how hopelessly frustrated and frightened Elena was, far away in Sydney, packing her bags. I felt so deeply for her, even as I watched her sister—my Cathy—confronting the demons of impending loss. "I know you are already grieving," I concluded. "All I have to do is look into your sister's green eyes to know a little of what you are feeling. We'll react to this carefully, a day at a time— making sure your dad doesn't feel a moment of loneliness at the loneliest moments of all. We'll all do what we can, knowing that the person who has the greatest burden is Marty himself."

Weeks later, in the steam of August, we all sat at the foot of Marty's reclining chair in Columbus. He was haggard, pale, still determined to manage his life. We wanted to talk with him. We did not want to misguide him into thinking that everything was all right, because it was not. We wanted to convey our concern and awareness of his limited prospects, without denying him his self-respect. The doctors had told him something ominous about his prognosis. He did not want us to ask him about the doctors, but we needed some guidepost to help plan for the next few weeks, or days. We understood that revealing to us what the doctors said would force Marty to surrender control of his waning life. He reacted harshly when asked what the doctors had shared: "There are options. Look, they say that I don't have unlimited time. I accept all of this. I'm not mad at God."

"Dad," I asked, "how much time do *you* think you have, and is there anything you want to tell us to do?"

"I think I have less than a year. And I want you to make Mother stop trying to get me to eat when I don't feel like eating."

His assessment proved wrong (he was gone in a month), and his protest about my mother-in-law was unfair and plaintive. But Marty was finishing as he had begun and as he had continued—thoroughly himself and thoroughly governing. Along with the rest of us, Elena bravely listened, holding her counsel, but not her love.

"There are millions of people," writes Dr. Elisabeth Kübler-Ross, "who still have the illusion that a patient is 'better off' if surrounded with an air of 'all is well'; that is, if we visit terminally ill patients only with a smile on our face and cheerful, superficial conversation. . . . We have no problems getting them the very best in physical care and attention, but most often neglect their more painful and spiritual turmoil." I think that the best way to interact with a dying person is not to be disingenuous about the whole thing, to offer support, and not to presume too much. The person you are visiting will usually set the tone; his or her condition has already set the agenda.

A friend came to visit Emma Bennett three months after Emma's surgery and diagnosis. "For some reason," Emma would write in her journal, "she thought that I would be in terrible shape. 'I've always been afraid to visit a cancer patient,' she said quite candidly. I didn't ask why. I just tried to make her comfortable."

Emma said that her friend, Susie, was really quite uncomfortable during the visit. But Emma still complained to Susie that she felt isolated from her friends. "I told her that I wanted to know what's going on in their lives. I need to feel that I'm still part of the world even if I don't do the things I used to do."

Emma mused that it was her broadcasting career that gave her insight on how to converse with others. "I learned how to listen to get the most information," she stated. "Let the person talk and before you know it, he will tell you more than he even intended."

But now, Emma was no longer in her television studio. She was at home, sick, and she wanted her friends to be themselves around her. Emma, terminal, yet still advocating for the other person in a room, concluded: "If you want to be a good friend to a cancer patient, listen. As a friend of a cancer patient, you should try to understand her feelings."

Wasn't Emma describing any person who is a friend of the living?

Chapter Seven

Even Death Honors Creativity

God created the world, but people are creating it.
—Rabbinic tradition

On Sunday evening, January 19, 1997, William Jefferson Clinton attended a Washington gala highlighting that weekend's inauguration ceremonies. Mr. Clinton was going to be sworn the next morning at the Capitol to begin his second term as President of the United States.

Backstage this Sunday night, technicians and entertainers were hurrying about, preparing for the nationwide telecast of the pre-inauguration function on CBS. One of the performers, then a forty-two-year-old veteran Broadway and cabaret singer, girded herself for a great and stellar moment: She would sing a song, backed by a huge chorus, to conclude and keynote this extraordinary event. She would then formally introduce the President of the United States.

Laurie Beechman came to this Washington zenith across a long road of sequential Broadway triumphs, professional awards, critical accolades, four compact disc recordings, and one defining illness. It was, in fact, her powerfully poignant album of hopeful ballads called *No One Is Alone*, released a few weeks prior to the President's party, that especially captured her brave and indomitable outlook on life and creativity. Beechman had survived for several years with ovarian cancer. She underwent a myriad of surgeries, treatments, and recoveries while continuing to make music. Just days before the inauguration, a producer associated with this CBS telecast, who had not known Beechman, found himself captivated by her rendition on that album of a hymn entitled "You'll Never Walk Alone."

Beechman, who I met at the time of her 1982 Broadway starring debut as The Narrator in *Joseph and the Amazing Technicolor Dreamcoat*, told me that she got the call at her home in suburban New York: "We are seriously considering having you sing that song for the President."

True to herself, and completely up to the task, Laurie responded: "What can I do to help make this happen?"

There was nothing in particular that she had to do. The producers knew of Beechman's record-breaking stint performing the unforgettable "Memory" as Grizabella in *Cats*; her starring role in *Les Misérables*; her appearance in the motion picture *Hair*; and her many celebrated television performances. They were undoubtedly cognizant of Beechman's solo presentation in Washington before Lady Margaret Thatcher, in honor of the former Prime Minister's birthday. They might have known about how, in 1977, as a young, unknown, wide-eyed contralto from Philadelphia, she stole the show, combining five roles and belting out "NYC" in the original Broadway production of *Annie*. Perhaps they were mindful, as her friends and family surely were, of how her struggle with a sinister cancer had deepened her voice, her heart, her soul. They likely surmised, being human themselves, that this remarkable woman would inspire the President's national audience as a teacher of mortality.

The inauguration festivities for a president surely yield a sense of history. Ascendant men and women gather to speculate, observe, record, and capitalize amidst this singular convergence of pomp, hegemony, ritual, and national succession. There is a sweeping dynamic of continuity and endowment. It is easy to forget that, beyond the protocol, beyond the institutional procedures, and the solemn promises made on Scripture, mortal men and women are simply gathering to shine and prosper for a sublime yet brief intersection of time, circumstance, and democratic will. It is impressive, important, and fleeting.

The legislators, ambassadors, cabinet officers, commentators, and other magnates who gathered in Washington for Bill Clinton's second installation may have felt a temporal sensation of immortality. Political and judicial events would come to demonstrate their collective frailty. But, that night, the air pure with the effervescence of a new term, the giants of dominion found themselves affected by something personal. When Laurie Beechman rose to chant about loneliness and courage, only the most jaded among them did not feel some inner tenderness beneath the glittering surface.

They knew from the video presentation preceding Beechman's rendition, which especially revealed her husband's extraordinary dedication to her, that she was fighting for her life, and that this was her song to being. For a moment, they forgot their high stations, their social guises, their political vizards. Perhaps they realized that even sovereigns and prelates live and die under the heaven; at the apex of power, they felt their undeniable, common vulnerability.

Laurie sang from deep within herself. Her sonorous voice rang through the immense hall; it was, to borrow a biblical phrase, like honey from a rock. Hard-boiled officials and sundry celebrities wiped their eyes and held their breaths. Laurie concluded her song; the huge chorus behind her withdrew from the stage. The audience stood in thunderous and sustained ovation. Beechman's heart pounded as she announced: "Ladies and gentlemen, the President of the United States!" Bill Clinton emerged, congratulating and embracing the exhilarated chanteuse. They parted, each to a different road down a corresponding journey.

What gave her such strength and such poise? How did she convert her life-threatening illness into an expression of life-affirming confidence? The answers have something to do with her view of mortality; unlike many people her age, she had been forced, several years earlier, to subject her existence to some earnest reflection.

For Beechman, it was not going to be the question of her death; it was going to be the answer of her life. Following the diagnosis of the cancer, which literally pulled her off a performance stage in 1988, she certainly passed through bouts of physical and spiritual duress. A burgeoning career was unquestionably diverted; it would, fittingly, be lifted soon enough by her acquired wisdom and her plain bravery. Inspirited by her family, especially her mother, Laurie did not permit her illness to distract from her inner commitment to artistry. "You are going through this," her mother told her, "because you are special." The young woman suffered through an arduous cycle of operations, chemotherapies, nausea, hair loss, remissions, and recurrences. Through it all, she recorded albums, appeared frequently on Broadway, inspired others who also were challenged by cancer, and gracefully accepted the exaltation of most of her peers, and the rejection of others who either wouldn't cast her or who figured, fallaciously, that she could no longer perform. "You are special," her mother told her, in the course of long, ardent, profound phone calls and conversations that took place so often during the years after the original diagnosis. "Special people are tested, for some reason."

Her mother told me that, once, when yet another watershed CT scan loomed, Laurie said: "Look, whatever they say now, I'll face it with dignity." She accepted, but did not acquiesce to the affliction. It's not that Beechman was given to emotional starch concerning her plight. She cried plenty, and she railed against fate and the attendant unfairness of the situation. Yet, ultimately, she returned again and again to her creativity. "What I want is normal," Laurie once told me about her view of living and loving. And what was normal for her was to make music. Whenever Laurie sang, she was spiritually protected against the encroachment of her mortal predicament.

I think that what heightens our fears regarding our mortality is the overwhelming loneliness that accompanies those fears. The prospect of death is a lonely one, indeed. You imagine yourself, first of all, sealed off from the universe. The contemplation of death can be peaceful and numinous, but it often sweeps us into a solitary emotional cubicle that is threatening and dark. Loneliness is a real attribute of our apprehensions; we anticipate being isolated and we struggle through this essentially alone with our thoughts.

I believe that even God was once lonely in the dusky and lifeless universe; that's why God began to create the world. In the activity of creating, God found relief and solace. Laurie Beechman, melody-maker to the Prime Minister and the President, found a balm for her loneliness by remaining artistic throughout her remaining life. Finally, toward the end, as her life began to recede, a family member remarked to me, with both pain and insight: "She has lived more in these last nine years than most people live in a lifetime. She just never stopped singing."

There is some peace to be made, even when facing mortality, by responding with creativity. Every person has some sort of skill or talent or ability. For some, it may be song; for others, weaving; for others, cooking; for others, model building; for others, teaching; for others, gardening; for others, mechanics; for yet others, the simple enjoyment of conversation. It doesn't matter what or how we create. The results are subjective, personal, and, often enough, redeeming. I learned from Laurie Beechman that, when facing mortality, a person might turn to his or her special capability—whatever that may be. When we create, we make light—even out of the greatest darkness.

I also learned from her not to feel sorry for myself when things that are really little take on big proportions. What a shame when people waste time being focused on trivialities. Every moment under heaven is a gift yearning for our gifts.

Dave Davenport did not look like he was born to be a banker. The chairman of the Security Bank sat behind his desk like a tiger in a cage. The strapping executive with the big, weathered hands and the blunt, sunburned face looked considerably younger than his sixty years. Yet, constantly a nurturing elder for younger people, he spoke with a disarmingly soft voice, telling me on one occasion: "Look, you have to build up your assets, and I want you to be smart with your money. But you have to take a vacation once or twice a year, so build some savings in just for that purpose. Nobody can function year-round without some time off from the grind."

Men and women of means and renown would come to see Dave at the unpretentious bank of which he was the founding father. Pampered, corporate types were drawn to this sanguine, urban frontiersman with the closely cropped whitish hair, the angular chin, and the muscular arms that lay across the desk like two shirt-sleeved logs. He was born in 1930, "during the Long Weekend," he liked to recount, in between the two great wars, much closer to poverty than to prosperity. He was reared in the projects, and he was always certain, while making his own, deliberate way up the ladder of civilization, of his own pulse. "My beginnings are important to me," Dave said. "I appreciate every dollar I've ever earned—not like some of these folks who come through here and take it for granted."

How I loved coming to sit and talk with this restless, brawny, quintessential American man. He enjoyed it when one day I told him: "Dave, it's too bad you weren't born a Jew." He laughed heartily, making sure, however, that I knew he received my remark as an exaltation. "Tell me some wisdom from your tradition," he challenged me. I quoted the Talmudic teacher, Hillel, for my friend and mentor: "In a place where there are no men, you strive to be a man."

Dave liked that, and he understood that I was talking about him. His gray eyes twinkled. He leaned forward, panther-like, his broad chest shoving the defenseless desk a bit in my direction. "I am a Jew. I am a Christian. I am a Muslim. God doesn't choose these notions. Only people do."

I was sure that if God needed a mortgage, he'd come to Dave Davenport.

Although Dave collected friends, he was, I thought, somewhat solitary. His marriage had stalled many years before; he was not blessed with good family relationships. His daughter, Edie, rarely spoke to Dave, even though he did see and spoil his grandchildren. He and his son, Dave, Jr., who also worked in the bank, agreed to a kind of emotional stalemate. The husky man who hunted elk during his retreats to a Canadian cabin felt more at home in the wilderness than in his own house. Meanwhile, he created a world for himself at the bank that he had designed and nurtured.

There was a certain, sweet sadness in him; he truly helped a lot of other people—primarily business associates and clients—achieve their goals while never quite finding his own peace of mind. Part of it was his take on most of humanity: He was not completely trusting, and he made himself more than a few enemies. Not everyone in the larger financial affairs community appreciated an aggressive little bank that sought to treat customers personally and that deliberately eschewed a corporate edge. "Every person who walks in here," declared Dave Davenport, "is a story. We'd like to get to know them, and work with them from that point of view." Dave meant it—that was his proficiency.

One day he phoned me and asked if I could stop by the bank. "I just want to talk with you a little bit. I have some religious questions."

I brought lunch over in a brown bag the next afternoon. Dave had no patience for business lunches out of the office. "Too much small talk, and too many calories," he would say, although he did have an occasional weakness for one exclusive Italian restaurant that served a particular clam sauce "that I would kill for."

Now I was thrilled that Dave had invited me to chat. We did this from time to time, philosophically combining themes of the bank and the Bible in ways that restored my perception of the simpler America my own immigrant father had chosen a generation prior. It was not lost on me that Dave Davenport and my father were both born in the same year, 1930.

I did not perceive his inner anguish when he asked me that day: "So how does a person know if he's left a mark in the world?" I was certain that Dave was just musing, as he often did, about the difficulty a man has in trying to stand out in this crowded and stressful society. Dave refused to accept the vacuousness of contemporary life; the malls, the cellular connections, the fax machines confounded him. He never would have adjusted to the cybernetic dispatch of e-mail. He saw in these conveniences the softening of the national spirit; he longed for the quiet dignity of a conversation, person-to-person, and he preferred such contact to any coaxial bit of interfacing.

I did not understand that day, or perhaps I refused to understand, that Dave was trying to tell me that he was sick. I just looked at him, sitting there regally in one of his wool sweaters (he kept a suit at the bank but rarely wore it), and I rambled on a bit. I knew that the world according to Dave Davenport was painfully inadequate. I said: "You have already made your mark. You have this mission to get others to build, and ponder, and fight. You get younger people to dream. You've left a lot of marks on plenty of people's lives."

"Yeah, but I wish I could do that with my own kids." I heard a melancholy strain in his voice, but dismissed it as one of his moods. Dave was infallible, as far as I was concerned.

The next time I saw him was in the hospital. The peculiar malignancy had blazed a trail between his right eye and that crooked nose of his. Dave lay there, as shrunken as I was disbelieving. "You didn't get it, Ben," he chastised me with a smile. "I'm going to be okay with this. I know I'm going to suffer a while, and then I'm going to die. I don't want any of those damned treatments. I don't need any more poison than the world has already dealt out. I'm okay with this. I just want to make sure that you are."

I was not okay with it. Dave's nose started to bleed. I took a towel and pressed it gently against his fragile cheekbone. When a nurse came, I fled the room, went out to the hospital yard, and wept like a boy who was losing his father. I wept because I was grieving for a man I had converted into an idol, even though he had discouraged exactly that kind of adulation. I wept because I understood that once in a while we are all lucky enough to meet somebody who can teach you something about how to live and something else about how to die.

The Very Reverend Joseph Jon Bruno's official title is Provost of the Cathedral Center of St. Paul and Pastor to the Congregation of St. Athanasius. Bruno is an Episcopal priest in Los Angeles with a unique background: For nearly six years, he was a Los Angeles city police officer, where he worked in vice, narcotics, undercover, and gang diversion. Not unlike Detective Dana Belmont (whom we met in Chapter Four), he has lived with the rough edges of mortality, and he has taken a human life. He maintains that he had an experience in the early 1970s "that would change my life forever."

After a period of service in the vice and narcotics section of the force, Bruno, a hefty man with strong, princely features, returned to the patrol division. There had been a kidnapping, and Bruno was assigned at the scene to take charge of the victim, who had been bound and gagged but managed to elude his captor. "After a short conversation with this individual," Bruno said, "I realized that his

captor was one of the people I worked on during my time undercover. I was ordered, since I knew this person, to set up a stakeout of
the site and wait for his return."

Bruno, the holder of three martial arts black belts, was nonetheless quite leery of this arrangement: "My supervisor was insistent that
I stay, even though the suspect knew me and I knew that he always
carried a nine-millimeter weapon. I had been in his home for dinner,
bounced his kids on my knee. I knew he would feel betrayed when
he heard my voice or saw me."

When the suspect returned, Bruno ordered him to lay down his
gun and surrender. "Immediately upon hearing my voice, you could
see by his eyes that he knew it was me. He took two shots at my
voice, one missed and the other just singed my hair." One of Bruno's
partners shined a light on the culprit, exacerbating the situation. "I
no longer had the luxury of playing with only my own life," said
Bruno. "As the suspect pointed his gun at the light and my partner, I
killed him."

The future cleric now found himself with blood on his hands. He
fell into a long and penetrating remorse, questioning his right to
adjudicate life and death. "The next year brought nightmares, justification by a coroner's inquest, and many attempts to free myself from
this burden." It may not surprise the reader that Bruno found eventual consolation through his faith in God. Confronted regularly with
nocturnal panic, cold sweats, and debilitating guilt, the big man
struggled through a mortality crisis gone unhinged. Every one of us
passes through something like this at some point and at some level.
We suddenly find ourselves alone in the throes of dread and realization: I am mortal, I am going to die. I am not invincible. I am going
to end and disappear from the face of the earth. For Jon Bruno, the
taking of a life so violently raised this latent human fear to the surface and unleashed it with unmerciful fury.

"For me," he reported, "it was the complete contradiction. I
believed that life was precious, and now I was a murderer." Bruno
knew intellectually that his had been a necessary and appropriate
response, and that he had been vindicated by the authorities. But the

fact of human mortality and its ramifications for the spirit are not always subject to reason and legalities. Guided by a sympathetic and intuitive priest, Bruno went and offered a confession for what he *felt* he had done—a murder. Through his prayers, he released the inner venom that was consuming him. A little bit of faith can mitigate the darkness of the night.

"I finally was blessed by a peaceful night without the terror," said Bruno. "The only thing that was able to help was that experience of confession and the assurance of God's forgiveness and absolution. Not that it made my actions correct or wiped out the pain, rather that there was a vehicle back to the presence of God."

Now, most of us will not find ourselves in Bruno's position— forced to subtract a human life. Nor are most of us consumed enough by theological passion to take up positions in the clergy. But none of us is immune from the fears of our finitude, and every single one of us is trying to make peace with mortality. A seasoned individual like Jon Bruno might certainly teach us that some level of personal spirituality can help restore the balance. "It brought my own mortality," now says the revitalized priest, "to a place of focus and reality."

The Reverend Bruno has seen a lot and his personal history is hardly devoid of exposure to the limitations and failures of human life. "I personally know, with daily reminders, how important life is and how fragile it is. My combined experience has brought me to a place where I try to use the baptismal convenant to teach that we must work for justice and peace. We must strive to respect the dignity of every human being."

From this knowing and tested soldier I learned that mortality is not just the manifestation of sick or older people who are getting ready to die. It is the delicate, constant denominator of our existence on the earth. If life is water, mortality is its tea bag. Jon Bruno, a child of East Los Angeles, a man who straddles the worlds of justice and holiness, a social worker who has held dying children in his thick arms, a priest who still attends to acts of violence in our streets and homes, has a mission: To restore the awareness of mortality to a sanctified place in our civilization. "You have only one choice and that is being a catalyst of change," he told me. "We, the religious leaders, have the only key that will fit the lock." That effort is Jon Bruno's art, and his creativity—preserving and fostering life at the edges of death.

During a resplendent luncheon in Atlanta, a young woman who knew something about life got up to tell her story. It was February of 1998, and Sarah Levin was in her freshman year of studies at Emory University. She was chosen to address this Children's Legacy gathering because she had suffered through a very serious illness and had lived to appreciate her developing experience on earth like few other teenagers ever had.

Sarah was only four years old when her parents already faced the fact that she was afflicted with something. Doctors declared that she had ulcerative colitis. She lived with the condition, however, up through the start of her teenage years. But when she was fifteen, she realized that things were not quite right. At the age when most people feel invincible, Sarah felt her energy wane, her weight drop, her drive fettered. She had to deal with the frequent questions of her teachers: "Are you okay?" The genial and idealistic dancer, figure skater, and musician knew that she wasn't feeling like herself. She said: "The smooth, four-year waltz down the yellow brick road began to take some detours toward the end of my sophomore year."

Even though Sarah continued to ice skate, run track, and play lacrosse, she knew that she wasn't all right. The emerging malady began to take over; she was forced to undergo a colectomy during her junior year. Complications ensued, and, just five days later, she underwent a second, emergency surgery. She wound up missing over two months of school, making up her work with tutors at home and a distinctively affirmative attitude within herself. My visits with Sarah were inspirational; I told my own teenage daughters (who know and admire Sarah) about what I learned from her. Levin's courageous brush with mortality has certainly been an indirect moral force in my children's lives, teaching them about priorities and values.

But Sarah still had a few more critical battles ahead of her. As her senior year in high school began, she withstood what can only be described as a near-death experience. As an outgrowth of a change in her medication, she had a reaction that suppressed her immune system. Lingering in the intensive care unit for five frightening days, she fought off the possibly fatal implications of septic shock syndrome—a deadly bacterial infection. At the luncheon this day in Atlanta, Sarah told a spellbound crowd: "I developed heart, lung, liver, pancreas, and kidney problems, as well as the inability to produce platelets. I had five blood transfusions. Fortunately, after five days, I began to turn around, slowly but surely. When I was finally able to return home, I realized how lucky I truly was to be alive."

Of course, Sarah's parents suffered through all of this, taking every precious breath with her, knowing her every stab of pain and cry of distress. Sarah held her own in between the shadows.

A peculiar twist of this episode was that, in its aftermath, Sarah and her family learned that the original, childhood diagnosis of colitis was actually incorrect. Sarah's condition was, in fact, Crohn's disease. She entered Emory University in the fall of 1997 and won a prize known as the Great Comebacks Award. Her condition steadily improved, and this young, self-effacing teacher of mortality now espouses the celebration of small triumphs. Her message resonates among other teenagers who are willing to listen: "I treasure each and every day."

Sarah thinks that one's experiences, especially the tribulations, leaven life. She has responded with her own unique artistry. Five hospitalizations and a serious brush with death have made her think a great deal about her unfolding career: She plans to become a child psychologist working especially with young people who are forced to spend a lot of time living in hospitals. Meanwhile, Sarah just plans on making music with her oboe, in-line skating, helping to build houses for Habitat for Humanity, working in hunger centers, and basically living without fanfare. "I just want to be normal," she said to her listeners in Atlanta, who understood that they were beholding a young woman who had *created* a distinguished normalcy for herself.

"I never realized," Sarah told me, "that people think I've accomplished so much. I feel like it's just been my life and I've had to deal with it just as everyone else must deal with what comes their way."

No wonder a group of nice folks in Atlanta invited Sarah Levin to
come have lunch.

Rena Moss was about the same age that Sarah Levin was at the
time of that Atlanta repast when Rena found herself with a different
kind of affliction. Nobody in Warsaw, Poland, Rena's home, was
inviting the young woman to a meal in 1939. When Rena and her
brother and sister were little children in Warsaw, it was a city brimming with Jewish life, filled with Yiddish gossip and Talmudic dignity. Now, as the Germans came with the shocking bacteria of hate,
the magic of Warsaw evaporated into the coming kingdom of death.
Late in 1996, I saw Rena as she lay dying in a hospice situated literally at the edge of Lake Erie. Water, foam, and eternity flapped
against the shoreline just outside the old woman's window. She was
no longer verbal, but her pretty face communicated a lot about her
long and sometimes frightful journey.

"She used to pull my long hair back from my face," said Simone,
her daughter, who stood by the bed. "Then she did the same thing to
my own daughter." I learned that Rena, who survived the Germans,
the postwar Displaced Persons camps, and a freedom trek to Israel,
never spoke much about the travails of her life. She just kept stroking
and caressing the cheeks, the eyes, and the foreheads of her descen-
dants. In this case, survival itself was the creative response to the
dominion of death. When Rena found herself struggling, at a ripe
age, with a terminal illness, she came to the lakeshore to die peacefully. It was clear that the feat of living long enough in the twentieth
century to die of a natural ailment gave her a certain satisfaction. Her
life had been scheduled to end two generations prior, when Warsaw
became a place for a Jewish teenager not to speak at a banquet but to
stake out a piece of stale bread.

"She made me what I am," said Simone. Having seen the brutality
of a few men directed against so many innocent people, Rena Moss
endured with the conviction that women should demand equality.
She gladly sewed her grandchildren's jeans, and she created a sizzling and nourishing matzoh ball soup for her family, but she taught
Simone to be physically agile and intellectually commensurate with

her male counterparts. "My mother was anything but frail," said the long-haired daughter of the survivor. "She was ravaged in the concentration camps, interned on Cyprus after the war, caught up in the struggle for Israel's independence. Somehow, through all the meanness, and hostility, and intolerance that she suffered at a young age, she was all about compassion and goodness."

Indeed, Rena gave birth to Simone's older brother, Abe, after arriving as an exile in the newly independent Israel. What better way to respond to murder than to create new life? Their taciturn mother taught her son and daughter a great deal about the gift of life. When she died, her children told the friends gathered at Rena's funeral: "We feel compelled to say something to commemorate, not the dreadful loss we now feel, but the gift of her life that will live forever in ourselves, her grandchildren and the grandchildren to come." Abe and Simone, who, according to Nazi blueprints, should never have existed, dedicate the poem "Desiderata" in memory of their mother:

> Go placidly amid the noise and the haste, and remember what peace there may be in silence. . . . You are a child of the universe no less than the trees and the stars; you have a right to be here. And whether or not it is clear to you, no doubt the universe is unfolding as it should.

"Nobody could wear a hat like Annie," said Carl about his beloved Anneliese. Annie had also survived the Holocaust, and emerged from Berlin and then wartime France with exquisite taste, dancing legs, mouth-watering recipes, an ear for music, and an eye for elegant art. As a teenager, she outlived the detention horrors at Gurs, lost both her parents, escaped into the French countryside, and found her way to America and into the arms of her future husband. She responded to all of it with an inventive commitment to life and without a trace of guile. On a sizzling July day in 1996, Annie, who reminded many of Audrey Hepburn, succumbed at home after a long and heroic battle with cancer.

Once, before the illness began to drain her of her vitality, she told me: "Who has time for nonsense? My children have everything. A few of us survived to see it. Why do people waste time fighting with each other? You never saw such a fight as I saw when I was a child. Why do people who have plenty fight about nothing?"

There are some people who, cursed by bitter experience, and then blessed by an equivalent wisdom, truly know how to live. When I saw Annie dancing for the last time, she swayed with seductive grace, and she wore a magnificent hat. When I saw her for the very last time, she had no hat, and she had no hair. But her eyes were as clear as the sky, and she was just as smooth and stunning as she had been on the dance floor. When I walked out of her bedroom and told her children to come in and tell her good-bye, I wished that I might someday know the fathomless peace of those eyes that had seen things I and Annie's children could only imagine.

We human beings, alkaline, fragile, limited, are part of a natural process; we bend into the wind and we spill into the sea. Along the way, we meet other people, some whose very names we fail to learn or remember, who nonetheless live in our hearts, creating values, teaching us the bittersweet resonance of human life. The hagiographic recollection of them also reminds us of faded times and places—a poignant echo of when life was simpler, we were younger, and our elders were mightier.

It was the summer of 1961. My family and I lived in Israel, still among the "remnant" immigrant-survivors who had arrived since the end of the Second World War, and those, who, like ourselves, were native to the land. There are many fascinating, intricate personalities that I recall from those more innocent days, including Booki the bus dispatcher, Steiner the town hobo, Binstock the bookseller, and Reiner the ice cream vendor. And then there was the unnamed farmer whom we boys simply called the Sweet Old Man with the Funny Sun Hat.

He was always there, in the clay house just beyond the trees. I still think of him often, certain that he has been gathered to the winds, wondering if such a person even exists anymore in the world. The old man, sweet as the oranges in his tiny patch, seems as wistful a memory as the kind of Israel that he and I inhabited more than a generation ago.

My boyhood friend, Yosi, and I were nine years old. Like so many remembered neighborhoods, our little village of Kfar-Saba had not yet matured into the more urban conglomeration of condominiums and shopping plazas and traffic circles that it is today. Kfar-Saba still slept quietly at the edge of the Samarian Mountains in central Israel. The sun beat down on us, without rain, from spring till fall. Time floated by, in clouds that whispered of Bible heroes.

Across the quiet road from my grandmother's house (where our family lived) was a thicket of ancient trees that captured the imagination of two carefree boys. Yosi and I would cavort in our private forest and play in between long shafts of sunlight. The trees gave shade and they fostered dreams. A favorite pastime of ours was to converge upon the forest after a summer matinee at the little cinema not too far away. Almost always, we watched Johnny Weissmuller in *Tarzan* installments. The jungle adventures were subtitled in Hebrew; now Yosi would climb a sizable timber and belt out a Tarzan jungle call that betrayed his Russian intonations. We were happy and free, early on the arc of mortality, and we knew of the nice, aged neighbor at the other end of this magical grove.

The sweet old man had no wife, and he lived alone in his tiny house. The grown-ups around the village spoke in whispers about him, saying something about "the camps" and about a lost daughter, and other things that we did not quite grasp then. The old man always wore a beaten, wrinkled sun hat. It seemed to be a part of his body, and it hung over the front of his brown and weathered face. His eyes were like two little stars glowing under the funny sun hat. He had a few orange trees in the thicket, along the edge of the small field near his house.

From time to time, Yosi and I would climb into the orange trees that belonged to the old man. Surreptitiously, we would seize one or two of the oranges and enjoy their juices. Sometimes, if we could secure good footing, we would peel and eat the fruit while remaining perched in the tree like Tarzan's Jewish watchmen. We would wait for the sweet old man to acknowledge our petty larceny. This he did, with his bell.

The bell, attached to the clay dwelling, could not be seen from the orange trees. It was located behind the house. The old man would ring the bell every time, just to let us know that he was aware of our clandestine enjoyment of his fruits. Whenever the bell rang, Yosi and I would clap sticky hands, and we would feel that everything in the world was just fine.

One afternoon, Yosi and I were sitting in the trees, sharing an orange, watching the old man's house. We had been there for a while, but we had not heard the bell. The grove was still, except for the muffled groaning of the city buses and the clicking of the horse-drawn wagons that traveled the road just beyond the edges of the forest. The humid air was thick with citrus smells, but no bell pierced the clearing. Yosi and I looked at each other, feeling a certain emptiness. We decided to descend and creep up close to the sweet old man's house.

Now we approached, squinting into his windows. We lived then in the world that came before the world of security codes, electronic fences, and domestic surveillance systems. A window was something you gazed through. "Look!" cried Yosi, in an excited gasp. There, sitting on an oak table, was the funny sun hat. It was like a cat, asleep and peaceful. Where was the old man? We tiptoed around to the next window portal.

"There you are, you two little outlaws!" The old man was laughing as he saw us from inside. He stood in his narrow kitchen, stirring something. "Come in, come in," he urged, laughing again. "I have something for you."

The sweet old man was stirring tea. The tea bags, like our little world, were scented with orange. On a large, round plate sat a stack of peanut cookies. "Look what I have for you two orange thieves who think I can't see you in my trees! Orange tea and cookies. Drink, boys, and feel welcome in my house."

We gathered at the oak table, peering at the crumpled sun hat. The old man brought out the tea kettle and a platter. Yosi and I saw that the oak table was covered with a long piece of glass. Under the glass was a host of pictures, all frayed with time. A handsome young man who strangely resembled our host held up a beautiful little girl with thick locks of hair in one of the larger photographs. A woman who clearly favored the little girl stood by, smiling. The setting behind and around all of them appeared to be a city far away; there were towering apartment buildings in the background that looked nothing like Kfar-Saba or even Tel Aviv. The woman and the girl appeared in most of the pictures under the glass. The old man ran his brownish fingers along the glass as he smiled at us. Then he poured the tea into glass cups. The cups, and his eyes, all brimmed with moisture.

The tea was warm, and we blew it cool. Yosi and I giggled with delight. The sweet old man was so gentle, and he even knew our names. We never even considered asking him his name—he was, indelibly, the Sweet Old Man with the Funny Sun Hat. "Listen, lads," he said, eyes shining again. "Leave me some oranges for the market! But come back every day."

We asked him: "Why didn't you ring the bell today?" I shall never forget his reply, which I have shared so often with my own children.

"It was time to see how much you cared."

It was on that day, from that lonely, kindly man that I learned about the best possible gift you get with this mortality, and that is the chance to invite somebody else into your soul. Meanwhile, the sweet old man's artistry was his resolute, blended harvesting of orange blossoms, survival, and memory. *God created the world, but people are creating it.*

"My life has been filled with challenge," Emma Bennett said, near the end of her useful and innovative life. She had seen so much, all of which she somehow turned to prudence. As a little girl in Canada, she watched her mother care for her natural father, her brother, and then her stepfather, all through their ailments and troubles. Life and circumstances were not easy in that time and place. Emma fretted deeply about her brother's family, particularly after her brother's son was killed in a school bus accident and his daughter was seriously injured in another mishap. Six months before Emma was to graduate with her degree, her own son was severely harmed in yet another accident. He lay comatose for three weeks; Emma nursed her son to recovery even as the doctors remained skeptical. She continued her own academic work for the full year afterward while her son recuperated and depended upon her at home. It seemed that many of the people close to Emma cried out to her in pain and need; she continued responding to such hurt while remaining focused on her own dreams. She had left Thorold, Ontario, while still in her teens, but it never quite departed from her.

"When my nursing career took a turn toward writing, I had decided I needed a liberal arts degree to become a more rounded person. Finding the time for a full-time job, family, and school took some creative shuffling, but I made it work. A brief internship at a radio station during a communications course turned into a job as an on-air personality—doing a medical program after graduation."

After her diagnosis of cancer, Emma wrote her personal story in a journal that combined biography, medical journalism, and the more delicate description of her forced transition from caregiver to care receiver. "There are days when I barely think about having cancer. . . . Life has changed for me since I was diagnosed. My tennis group still doesn't contact me. I was disappointed that twenty years with the same group of people meant so little to them."

Even around the patients she still served while being ill herself, Emma constantly fell back on her sunny, if realistic disposition. Stung by her tennis group's withdrawal, she turned in other directions: "I've developed new friendships and rediscovered old friends. What have I learned from all this? Life doesn't have to revolve around physical activities. My tennis group was just that—a group of people I played tennis with twice a week. Friendships are different."

Near the end of her days, at the close of her journal, Emma concluded: "I understand friendships now. There are all kinds—casual, close, permanent, temporary, and intermittent. They can all be good once we understand them. I was disappointed with my tennis group because I didn't understand the category. Now I consider myself lucky. I have a lot of friends in all the categories."

In classical literature, Plato quotes Socrates as saying that "those who really apply themselves to philosophy are directly and of their own accord preparing themselves for dying and death." Because our finitude can teach us about cherishing things, Wallace Stevens describes death as "the mother of beauty." But not only the exalted philosophers and poets understand the magnificent tyranny of living and dying; insight comes from the high winds and the distant river beds and the far-flung pagodas of human experience.

Up the road from Toronto and Haliburton, among the high pines of northern Ontario, Dorothy Nicholls sits in her summer cottage and scribbles a letter to me about her inspiring friend and relation, Emma Bennett: "Emma had a lot of life experiences and information to share, and she did that very well in all her endeavors. In the end, she taught us about life and how to leave it with dignity, and that we must face it together."

What Do We Get in Exchange for Death?

At the beginning of this book, I remembered the nobility of Mrs. Sally Mond, wife of the rabbi, who faced her imminent death with grace and assent. I recounted the sentiment we onlookers shared on the evening she visited a community wedding reception and bade us farewell, that Mrs. Mond taught us a great deal about making peace with mortality. Softly, delicately, self-effacingly, Mrs. Mond expressed her gratitude for this life and her acceptance of life's end. Now I wish to add: Many people present that night, touched by Sally Mond's courage, moved by Rabbi Mond's obvious despair, wondered to each other: Where do our beloved go after they leave us?

There are, of course, answers to this that come from virtually every tradition. The Hopi Indians tied prayer feathers to the feet and the hands of their deceased and covered the lifeless face with a cloud-like flower of raw cotton that symbolized the heavens. The Hopis placed a secure stick in the grave to serve as a ladder for the spirit to climb and depart to the west, which was the home of the ancestors. It doesn't matter who you are or what you are: We human beings imagine and wonder and ache for the knowledge of where our journey leads, and where our beloved reside.

The Jews generally yearn eastward for sanctification. The Chinese believe in the eternal circle; the followers of Zoroastrianism dream of the Chivnat Bridge over which the dead cross into paradise. The African peoples, though drawn from many cultures, share a common belief in a natural journey: The dead transition from the physical world that we see into a union with creation itself. The Hindus and the Buddhists feel a peace in the processes of life; those who live well and wisely, they maintain, are reincarnated, blessing this realm again with their wisdom and insight.

So one thing that we get in exchange for death is faith. The two crave one another; in so many ways, it is death that bequeaths God. And no matter what the lyrics or variations are of anybody's personal creed, it is the fact of death that makes the prayers real. Heaven has been enshrined in countless, disparate poems and liturgies; there would be no reason for heaven if there wasn't the unifying inspiration of mortality.

But, meanwhile, I never thought that the fragile Mrs. Mond crossed any rivers or made her way into the horizon. My own tradition generally has no specific destinations or locations or even chemical properties associated with our beloved who have died, except that it asserts an absolute belief in the eternity of the human soul. We don't get too philosophical about it because, one, we emphasize what to do with *this* life, and two, we are basically a pragmatic people who believe in what we see and have faith in what we don't.

But I know that Rabbi Mond must have wondered, time and again, where his wife was. I am certain that he yearned for some intuition, some sense as to how he could find her in his longings and his loneliness, his own struggle with mortality. Who among us has not known this anguish, not searched this path?

When my father-in-law, whom I have written about in this book, died, I myself found that the standard answers, the kind rituals, even the comforting words of others went some way toward helping with our family pain. But they did not succeed in directing us all the way. I found myself wanting the same answer that so many people have inquired of me over these years: Where is my loved one?

It wasn't always enough, I discovered, to hear that he was "in a better place." Tender, generous, clean was this response, but it really was the answer of the sympathetic visitor who didn't really know where my lost one was, and therefore offered a humane supposition on the matter of eternity.

I found myself hoping, after experiencing that death in our family, that I had not too often responded to other people's sorrow and needs with some well-meaning but opaque guess about where a departed person now is. I suppose one's own bereavement tightens the lining of the soul, and we are raw with criticism and angry from grief when losing someone special. But many years ago, a rabbi I admired lost his wife, and I heard people rejoin with pat answers. As stated earlier, I think that people who haven't suffered mean well, but people who have suffered mean business.

Now, given fresh insight by our own sadness, my family sought to transcend the formulas and find the answer to where our dear one had gone and to where *we* go after fulfilling this life. I have found the answer, and—though different from the visions of holy rivers, star-borne journeys, blessed sticks, or ethereal bridges—it lives in the same place as all these articles of faith. I have found my loved ones, and not only the one lost most recently. I have found them—*they are located directly in my heart.*

Mortality mingles souls. It tempers arrogance, and, when accepted and understood, brings tender insight. A friend of mine, Mary Anne, has known more than her share of deaths and troubles. A gifted journalist, she has rubbed shoulders with a number of celebrated editors and subjects. But what she has rubbed against most is the acknowledgment of life's lessons.

"I was the fifth child of my parents and the first girl," she told me. "I was sandwiched between the deaths of two boys, one a Down Syndrome baby who was sent to a 'home' because relatives determined that was the best for my rather sickly mother and my overwhelmed father, and a twelve-pound baby boy who died due to being poisoned by the medicine for my mother's kidney ailment."

Mary Anne's parents were devout and institutional Catholics. "I do know that I have a faith in God but not the way the nuns taught me. I strongly relate to faith as a part of my being and not as a ritual." Mary Anne has a right to examine her theology because she has passed through several crucibles and has emerged with a quiet outlook about mortality: "I do believe we can bear what happens to us."

She remembers her oldest brother, Bryan, "a great athlete and the most handsome of my brothers," being struck down by epilepsy at the age of thirteen and then suffering through fifteen years of cancer treatment. She recalls her "favorite cousin," Tim, an Air Force colonel, with whom she made a final pilgrimage to their ancestral Ireland. Tim, dying, came looking for his roots. There, in a rocky family cemetery, Mary Anne had scooped up some dirt and stones, hiding them away in a jar. At her cousin's subsequent funeral at the Air Force Academy, Mary Anne revealed the well-traveled jar, opened it, and sprinkled the dirt into the open Colorado grave of her "soul mate." Death, the magnificent tyranny, changes any place we cherish into holy ground; death bequeaths us heaven.

Mary Anne had next to deal with the serious stroke suffered by her husband Joe, a renowned Midwestern columnist and her very touchstone. Joe fought back to regain his strength, wit, and acumen. I asked Mary Anne how all of this has affected her.

"You asked how did these deaths—and Joe's brush with death—change me? I am still struggling with that. I think the most outward change is my lack of ambition and my yearning for quiet time to reflect. I truly enjoy my little cottage by the lake, a midday sail, a glass of wine, and yearn for a simple life." Something good and softening has happened to Mary Anne, as she finds herself along the path of the soul.

Mary Anne's eyes sparkled with joy and experience. She suddenly remembered something: "I wore blue and white until I was seven years old in honor of the Blessed Virgin."

So what now? I inquired.

"The girl in blue and white rarely goes to church though I fervently believe in God and goodness," said the journalist who has become first and foremost a daughter, wife, and friend. For her mortal experiences, Mary Anne has found out a lot about who she is.

What do we get in exchange for death? We get life . . . a vast panorama of possibilities and pathways. We get the sensation of taste and the satisfaction of ideas, the interesting development of personal growth, the beauty of intimacy with other people. We often get the gift of children and/or protégés, and we get the wisdom that risk and mistakes offer only to the human species.

We get the never-ending but fascinating mystery of the universe and its elusive yet comforting concept of a God. We get night yielding to day, rain pounding on our windows, and the bittersweet but uniquely human intuition that it all should be appreciated, revered, and measured because it is all framed in a process where life and death are inextricably and necessarily interwoven.

We get to love a few special people, and, if mortality calls them before it calls us, the honor of remembering them. Meanwhile, living a creative life that lifts the spiritual above the material helps assure that someday, somebody we touched will benefit from remembering us.